The Hooker's Daughter

A Boston Family's Saga

By

Dale Stanten

With

Rowena Winik

INFINITY
PUBLISHING

Copyright © 2010 by Dale Stanten

ISBN 0-7414-6402-0

Printed in the United States of America

Published February 2011

INFINITY PUBLISHING
1094 New DeHaven Street, Suite 100
West Conshohocken, PA 19428-2713
Toll-free (877) BUY BOOK
Local Phone (610) 941-9999
Fax (610) 941-9959
Info@buybooksontheweb.com
www.buybooksontheweb.com

For Randee and Dean

With All My Love

I've never tried to block out the memories of the past, even though some are painful. I don't understand people who hide from their past. Everything you live through helps to make you the person you are now.

—Sophia Loren

What goes on between a writer of personal true-life stories and the person who reads them is like a friendship – and real friendship is exchanging secrets, taking hostages, rolling over like a dog and exposing your soft throat.

—Adair Lara

The fathers have eaten sour grapes, and the children's teeth are set on edge.

—Jeremiah- Chapter 31-Verse 28

Prologue

Memories play maddening games. They torture with their elusiveness. When emotional resistance is low, they crowd in — unwanted and unwelcome — jostling for space. They line up with a beautiful logic one day, only to shift and reappear in absurd juxtaposition another day. My mind sometimes has trouble dispelling these tormentors and continually revisits them, looking for meaning. Should my children see me from that perspective which I have hidden for so many years? I was not a party to the behavior, but somehow I ended up owning it, and now feel compelled to rid myself of its taint by telling the truth as I know it. I have finally learned a degree of dispassion, and when the memories come crashing in like storm-driven waves, I watch them from a comfortable distance.

This book began with my efforts in a writing group which met in the back room of Swampscott's local Panera Bread bakery-café on Wednesday mornings. The group was both fascinated, shocked by my story as it emerged, and eagerly awaited each new installment. I was touched by this unselfish outpouring of interest and found welcomed motivation in their support.

1

After my initial attempts as a writer resulted in a working draft, my sister Rowena, offered to help me edit the work and recall more of the specific details of our early life. The collaboration grew beyond a writing partnership and the laughter, tears, and intense conversations gave way to a degree of self-awareness we had never experienced. Our separate memories of the early years proved to be similar, and that fact gave me the assurance that I was not embellishing the past with overwrought emotions and interpretations.

Two sisters' lives had been split apart by our parents' reprehensible actions, and for many years Rowena and I wrestled with the past separately, without the warmth and support of the other. The process of coming together to work on this book was an incredible opportunity and a gift, and I will be forever grateful to Rowena for her contributions.

I have taken the liberty to change a few names. If my recollections differ from anybody discussed in this memoir, I regret any unintended harm.

Part One

Ladybug! Ladybug!
Fly away home.
Your house is on fire.
And your children are gone.

All except one,
And that's little Ann,
For she crept under
The frying pan.

One

Ma was the center of our universe. We watched her, basked in her glory, abhorred what she did but ferociously protected her secrets, and waited anxiously to find out what misfortune her activities might visit upon us.

At the tender age of six, I understood that Ma was a hooker.

Though I may not have had a grasp of the details of what went on in the next room, by that age I had seen enough men in a state of arousal and sweaty anticipation to recognize that their presence in our apartment was at the core of an unsavory aspect of our existence.

Two

Ours was one of tens of thousands of families living in Boston's densely populated sister neighborhoods of Roxbury, Dorchester and Mattapan in the early 1940s and 50s. This was old Jewish Boston, a successful community comprised mainly of brick apartment buildings and two and three family wooden houses. The area teemed with the personality, enterprise, and vitality of its clannish Jewish residents.

By the mid 1960s racial block busting would precipitate a rapid decline in the Jewish population. However, while I was growing up there, life was a rich ethnic experience. The downside for our family was the rapidity with which gossip traveled among its denizens. Because of Ma's choice of profession, our family name of Winik was often on the tongues of neighbors and strangers—and not in a good way.

All types of storefront shops and stalls lined the Blue Hill Avenue corridor (disparagingly referred to by some as "Jew Hill Avenue") like an Oriental bazaar. I knew all of Ma's favorites, and earmarked each vendor's unique offerings for her scrutiny. While passing through the fish market, I slyly touched the scales of whole fish displayed on beds of cracked ice. At the grocer, I pointed to the kaleidoscopic heaps of dried apricots, prunes, raisins, pears, and nuts piled high in burlap bags, barrels or satchels, hoping Ma would pause there so we could pick through them.

As we walked by the Sunlight Bakery and caught a whiff of fresh baked bread, I tugged on Ma's jacket, hoping she would buy me a chocolate cupcake. Ma was generous about dispensing sweets, and I was seldom disappointed.

My sister Rowena, older than I by six and a half years, often took me by the hand and together we explored the legendary G&G Deli where throngs frequently gathered outside to listen to raucous political rallies. But the two of us had little interest in political enlightenment. Our sights were set on the two-inch corned beef sandwiches oozing mustard, and the aromatic barrels of mouth-watering kosher pickles that seemed to beckon to us from inside. The *kishke* (Eastern European sausage meat and grain) saturated in thick brown gravy was a big favorite. On Saturday nights, as part of our routine, we went to Eagerman's factory on Erie Street for freshly baked hot bagels.

We often lingered at the butcher shop window to watch the family of Orthodox butchers demonstrating their impressive skills on enormous sides of beef piled on bloody chopping blocks. On Friday nights, we observed the crowds of religious Jews, clad in their best, solemnly walking to Shabbat services at the many *shuls* (synagogues). During the Jewish high holidays of Rosh Hashanah and Yom Kippur, groups of teenagers congregated and schmoozed at "the Wall" in Franklin Field Park, a revered rite of passage. We had a sense of belonging by embracing the warmth of our customs and rituals.

Three

Ma was the first of two daughters born to Rose (Bubbe) and Grandpa David, both early-1900 émigrés from Eastern Europe who met and married in Boston. She was born in 1917 and given the name of May. Her sister, Helen, arrived ten years later. When Ma was a child and Auntie Helen still an infant, Grandpa David suddenly killed himself at the age of thirty-nine. He wrote a suicide note neatly in Yiddish on the back of a dry cleaning ticket and left it where it could be found. It was a puzzling and strangely unemotional note, revealing little of his state of mind or what unknown illness he may have had:

> *"My dear wife Raytze (Rose). Pay attention to the children. I am sick and I don't want to bother you. You will be better without me.*
>
> *— David"*

David's suicide dealt an enormous blow to Rose and her older daughter. The new widow struggled financially and passed on her intense worries about the family's financial future to May. As an impressionable young girl, the deep-seated terror of impending poverty may have been at the root of many of Ma's major life choices.

My mother claimed that Bubbe had been a slim, *frailich* (lively) and delicate beauty with a love of music and dancing. So it was not surprising that she remarried quickly after David's disturbing death and moved the little family to New York. But the marriage failed within a year, and Bubbe brought the two girls straight back to Boston where she struggled to make ends meet by taking in sewing and alterations. Although too young to work, Ma tried to help their desperate financial situation conserving electricity by bathing only in the dark and walking everywhere instead of taking the bus. Whether or not the little girl's self-imposed privations had any effect on the family's ability to save money, they certainly seem to have colored her perceptions.

Bubbe had a dramatically different set of expectations for each of her two daughters, and this was noticeable to everyone. She was tyrannical and unforgiving with May, who realized early that she could not please her mother no matter how hard she tried, but she indulged Helen and expected very little from her. Despite the startling inconsistency in her attentions to her daughters, Bubbe still managed to command the fierce devotion of both of them. Even when we were very young, Rowena and I understood the intensity of the bonds that held these three women in an unholy trinity. We knew we could not penetrate it, and so we simply accepted and went along with it.

As a general rule, Bubbe did not elicit warm, fuzzy feelings in me. She usually seemed irritable, and constantly complained about everything under the sun. It hurt me to see how tough she was on my mother and I was usually very wary in her presence. Faced with all of her rules and prohibitions, Rowena and I thought of her house as a never-never land—full of negatives. She forbade us to enter the living room—which was protected from all possible onslaughts by heavy duty plastic coverings on the sofas and chairs—and we were restricted to sitting at the kitchen table when visiting. I managed to get some rebellious thrills by sneaking into the living room for fast visits, just to outwit my controlling grandmother, but I was never caught in the act and never learned what the penalty might be for such mischief. If one of us wanted an apple, Bubbe had to be the one to open the icebox to get it. If we wanted glasses of water, she insisted on filling the glasses herself and handing them to us. Reacting against the strangest prohibition of all, we assiduously avoided ever using our grandmother's toilet because she insisted on flushing it herself after every use.

Bubbe had a robust enthusiasm for fun in spite of her often dour, critical manner. She loved dining out, going to Yiddish theater, leading her peers in Yiddish songs, and dancing. She was a marvelous cook, and often tried to manipulate Rowena and me into favoring her meals over our other grandmother, Mucky. Bubbe's meals were simple and light—delicate cheese blintzes, *varnishkas* (kasha with onions and bow tie pasta), and fluffy matzo balls accompanied by tiny cooked chicken egg yolks that floated in her chicken soup. Mucky's meals were hearty and heavy—brisket, potato pancakes, and *tsimmes* (combination of fruit, meat and carrots).To us, there could be no absolute winner—how do you choose between a bathing suit and a winter coat!

We were relieved that Ma had inherited Bubbe's desire for fun, and not the more cantankerous side of her nature. Ma often said "I want to dance at everyone's wedding and enjoy life!"

However, Ma did inherit a troubling tendency toward callousness.

I have a small collection of things I prize—a teddy bear, a red wagon, roller skates, and Rowena's hand-me-down bike—all of which supply me with countless hours of solitary diversion. One day, I come home from school to discover that my bike is gone.

"Ma , Ma, my bike is missing! Have you seen it?"

She nonchalantly replies, "You don't need it anymore, so I sold it and got $5."

That was definitely the Bubbe in Ma. Her insensitive act was confusing and I wondered if my mother cared about me at all. Did she forget that the bike was very important to me, especially because it had been Rowena's?

On the other hand, it was comforting when the soft side of Ma doted on me.

"Here," she murmurs with that guttural incantation I remember so well. "Come to bed, and I will rub your head and chant you to sleep. There, mein kindt (my child), doesn't that feel better?" Just as I am falling asleep to the sound of her comforting words, the tone of her voice changes to sadness and regret: "Ah, Dale, you must know I am sorry I hurt our family in so many ways. I didn't want to, but I had to do what I had to do. You know, I always had to be the one to keep the wolf from the door."

These words from the past remind me that she, too, was a victim. How many mothers before her allowed their actions to be shaped by the need to overcome hardship? I don't know the answer. But I see Ma as part of that continuum visited upon her by her own mother.

Four

My family lived in a three-story brick building in Mattapan which housed thirteen apartments. Our 1333 Blue Hill Avenue address was considered a respectable one with its very own irascible janitor, Karpo, who lived in a cheerless room in the cellar. I suspect he had other responsibilities besides shoveling coal into the furnace. He would shoo the kids away with a broom if we were in his way, and endlessly rolled his own cigarettes while sitting on the side of the building.

An inviting branch of the Boston Public Library was directly across the street from our apartment building and the elementary and junior high schools a short 5-10 minute walk. The streetcars, clanking on the tracks, ran regularly, enabling us to travel around the area quite easily, particularly to the treasured Franklin Park Zoo.

Vendors commonly delivered door-to-door—would it be the familiar Hood's milkman or a solicitation from Cushmans' with breads and pastries, spilling out of big baskets? Best of all were the Yiddish-speaking peddlers from the old country hawking wares. When one of those yarmulke-clad, chubby Santa figures approached our building urging, "Kafe, kafe" (buy, buy), my heart always pounded in excited anticipation. I wondered, what would be today's bounty hidden inside his leather satchel—the familiar cherry Life Savers, thread, aprons, shoelaces, dishtowels, or something completely new and exciting.

A hallway, poorly lit from the skylight above the third floor, led to our dark, pocket-sized three-and-a-half-room apartment, located on the first floor at the rear of the building. The tiny, windowless living room—originally intended as a simple vestibule—was furnished with a sofa, a green leather easy chair, a matching bridge chair, and a black lacquered cabinet adorned with Ma's prized *chotchkes* (knickknacks). If my father was at work, we had a chance to sit on the sofa. But, when he was home he stretched out on it like an invalid in a sick bed. In the evenings, he moved his feet so my mother could sit at one end.

We were the first family in the building to have television, a seven inch Garod. Ma occasionally invited the neighbors to bring their own chairs and watch *The Milton Berle Show*. She seemed oblivious to our cramped quarters and did her best to maintain order in such small space.

Anyone stepping into our apartment was surprised by our parents' fully displayed bed with its shiny powder blue satin bedspread. The French doors between their bedroom and the living room had been removed long ago by previous tenants, and for some reason, our parents never replaced them. The shock effect of entering our apartment and immediately seeing the bedroom was like mistakenly opening a door and seeing a naked person sitting on the toilet. There was simply no place for the eyes to shift, nothing to buffer the embarrassment. As Rowena and I grew older and more self-conscious, we dreaded the reaction of our friends when they first saw such a private place so crudely revealed to public view—especially when our parents were lying together in the bed.

The kitchen was a cheerier, more inviting place, and was often bathed in sunlight from two large windows. It was furnished with a maple breakfront in which a decorative dish collection was displayed. A rather pretentious Russian samovar, brought from the old country by Daddy's mother, sat on top of the refrigerator and peered haughtily down its spigot at Ma's plain old cast-iron potato baker, which was always on the stove. I felt a sense of contentment—often fleeting—as I leaned against the warmth of the sizzling radiator next to the dinner table.

Beyond the kitchen was a cluttered pantry where dishes were washed and canned goods lined the shelves. It led to the back porch and fire escape where Rowena and I often played together. Although there was no door between the pantry and the kitchen, it was in this teeny space where Ma conducted some of her business. She did not use the bedroom—too public, and no escape from instant discovery. In addition to the occasional use of the pantry, the bathroom was a busy place during Ma's hours of business. Because it had a door, it was a slightly less risky choice.

Our narrow bathroom had a single wall rack that displayed Ma's never-to-be-touched decorative guest towels. We used only the two raggedy, damp ones that were draped on the sides of our gritty bathtub. In addition to being used by all four of us, I assume they might also have been used by Ma's johns. Despite such heavy communal use, Ma sent those towels out only once a week with the rest of our laundry. We did not have the luxury of a washing machine or dryer.

My sister and I shared a small bedroom with twin beds that we regularly used as trampolines. Two dressers, a reading chair, a linoleum floor printed with game boards and a hopscotch layout completed our room. It also housed the apartment's only two closets, which barely handled our own storage demands, let alone Ma's. She was a clothes horse and had a very large wardrobe, but stored her clothes with ours, making the closet situation chaotic.

Ma kept our crowded apartment as neat and as attractive as she could under the circumstances, and was determined to view it through rose-colored glasses, imagining it as something better—a showplace imbued with highly attractive decorative features.

Five

It was an intimate conversation between two disappointed housewives that spawned the idea of turning tricks to make ends meet and got my mother started in her trade. Ma complained to her friend that Daddy's business was failing and she feared his scant earnings would quickly bring us to the edge of poverty, the thing she feared most. In turn, the friend confided that she had been "entertaining men" for some time, which supplemented the family income nicely.

Ma quickly became a true believer and instantly felt empowered by her new business. Traditional hardscrabble employment was for chumps—she was on the pathway to the big bucks! In her mind, this career choice was about basic survival for our family. But, in addition, she could buy things she never had, go places, and experience life the way she had always dreamed. She could also dress up in nice evening clothes, go out, dance to the current music, and meet men with similar tastes.

Before opening the door for business, she scoped out the neighborhood and planned an emergency escape route for the johns through the back porch. She reasoned that the twelve other apartments in the building would camouflage the conspicuous parade to and from our door. But clearly, few people were fooled! After all these years, I am still hearing from acquaintances that Ma's activities were common knowledge. She was infamous in our neighborhood—and beyond in the greater Boston vicinity. Ma was a real natural, and started raking in money immediately. Her busy schedule started early on weekdays with regular morning hours.

Ma's business is growing rapidly and I am still too young to go to school. She needs the apartment to herself in the mornings. To take care of this problem, she tells Rowena to take me with her to elementary school. "Smuggle her into the kindergarten, the teacher won't know the difference. Dale will blend in with the other kids."

Mortified, Rowena—only eleven years old—executes her mission. But shortly after classes begin, I am discovered and the principal calls Rowena to her office to take me home. Rowena— Ma's most loyal subject—takes full blame for the stowaway gambit. Ma is undaunted by Rowena's report on the failure of the mission and sends me back with her the next day when, of course, my presence is immediately discovered. The principal calls Ma and meets with the three of us in her office. Ma pretends it was all Rowena's idea and joins in the principal's scolding. Fast becoming a part of Rowena's conspiracy to protect our mother, I try my own infantile tactic and announce to the principal in my most threatening voice, "I'll eat that candy on your desk if you don't let me come to school!" To this day, I cannot look at a Hershey candy bar without thinking ruefully of that long-ago, strange, almost burlesque, farce.

When I was finally old enough to go to school, I developed a delaying routine to postpone Ma's morning appointments for a few more minutes. I dressed, changed and changed again, and then asked Ma's advice about the choice, but remained dissatisfied, no matter what. The push-pull with Ma made me insecure and I worried that she was mad at me. I generally stopped halfway to school, turned around, and ran home. Once home, I didn't dare go inside, but stood at the backyard window calling to her and begging forgiveness. Ma would appear at the window and assure me that she was not angry. Then she shooed me off to school in her familiar Yiddish, "*Gayshin mein kindt*" (go, my child). It became our quaint mother-daughter routine for a time.

If a john rang the doorbell before I left for school, Ma wrestled with the propriety of allowing him to enter our apartment.

One day after Daddy leaves for work, a john shows up.

"*Hey May, got a minute?*"

"*My daughter is still home. Can't you wait till she's gone?*"

"*Oh, come on May. I only have a short time. I'll have a little extra for you. What do you say?*"

"*It'll have to be quick.*"

"*OK*"

"*Dale, Go to your room.*"

I go to my temporary prison and close the door as Ma and the john disappear into the bathroom. After a few minutes I sneak out and hear grunting and groaning. I fling open the bathroom door and see them both on the floor. The john's pants are down to his ankles and Ma's skirt is hiked up.

I scream, "Stop it! What are you doing?"

Ma kicks the door shut.

I was hoping to shock her into calling a halt to things and sending the john away. But such crude, childish tactics always failed. Ma just ignored my tantrums. Soon the john was gone and I went off to school.

Six

May Mish graduated from Revere High School with enough bookkeeping skills to get an office job at City Hall. She told me on more than one occasion how proud she was to work there. Like all the other teens living in that North Shore beach town, she looked forward to spending summer weekends hanging out at Punk's Corner, the local gathering spot of teenagers.

In those days, Revere Beach was known as "the people's beach" because of its popularity with immigrants and working class people from nearby towns who flocked there for their vacation escapes. Unlike most beaches offering mainly sun, sand, and surf, the Revere Beach of that day was also crowded with amusements. Notable attractions included the Whip, a Ferris Wheel, Bluebeard's Palace, a Fun House, Hurley's Dodgems, the Hippodrome, the Virginia Reel, and the Cyclone, one of the largest roller coasters in the United States. Several local ballrooms were sites for the dance marathons that were all the rage in the 1930s. Roller skating rinks, bowling alleys and a dazzling assortment of food stands all thrived on that stretch of road along the beach.

One hot Sunday afternoon, a slender twenty-year-old stranger stepped out of the crowd at Punk's Corner, introduced himself to May, and handed her a package. Art Winik had purchased a birthday present for his girlfriend, but the two argued and broke up before he gave it to her. Out of spite, he decided to present it to the next girl he met. Enter spunky and pretty May, who happily accepted the gift as her due.

Art's "coke bottle" thick glasses, necessary to correct severely crossed eyes and poor vision, detracted from his overall appearance. However, he projected a self confident demeanor. It is easy to imagine why he was attracted to May, but her interest in him may have been motivated by his apparent financial stability. He worked in and expected to inherit his family's successful business.

The couple immediately began dating steadily, and when May, at the age of eighteen, became pregnant with Rowena, they married. By all accounts, Art and May were a spirited young couple with a large circle of friends. They visited each other's homes and enjoyed picnics in the park. On Sundays, they rode horses together in the Blue Hills Reservation near Boston.

Art was a skilled bowler with scores in the 200s and all his pals wanted him on their team. He routinely spent time at the racetracks until the day he squandered his diamond ring—a fiasco which put an abrupt end to this particular gambling habit.

May enjoyed card games and had an endless appetite for poker, which she played regularly with a group of girlfriends. She often joked about the group's addiction to the game and said they could play for two days running without even so much as taking bathroom breaks. According to her, the group would rather have peed in their chairs than leave the action even for a moment. Art also enjoyed a good card game and occasionally sat down with

May's group. Afterwards, the couple stayed up for hours happily recalling cards played, bets poorly placed, and money won or lost.

Daddy's parents, Mercka (Mary) and Sol Winik, were part of the wave of Yiddish-speaking Russian immigrants who arrived in the U.S. in the early 1900s. It was Rowena who, as a toddler, gave Mercka the nickname "Mucky," a name that stuck with her for the rest of her life.

She had once been beautiful in a Russian mujik sort of way. She was a stocky, strong woman, with a rough aura of one used to hard work and formidable challenges. But along with her physical toughness, Mucky had a loving and welcoming way, always willing to laugh and act like a kid right along with the rest of us. Ma herself appreciated and felt connected to Mucky's strength and adaptability because they were traits she herself possessed.

Before their oldest son was born, the Winiks worked unsparingly to develop a successful meat trucking company, which became their family business and employed two of their three sons until the end of World War II.

Daddy was the oldest and a typical kid who grew up loving the Boston sports teams and his dog. Mucky treated her sons as royalty, but it was Art who held the vaunted position of Crown Prince and got extra special consideration from her. She coddled and protected him from any criticism that came his way.

Becky (Ben), the middle brother, was a workhorse and, like Art, his basic good looks were marred by badly crossed eyes. Generally, he was reticent except when he was around his wife and four children. However, Becky was prone to occasional violent displays of temper, some of which likely sprang from irritation with his older brother's apathy and sense of entitlement.

Pasey (Paul), the youngest brother, had his own physical challenges to deal with. He contracted polio as a child and enrolled in ballroom dance classes to recover muscle strength and coordination. As his dancing skills progressed and his passion grew, Pasey became known publicly as "the teenage Fred Astaire."

He teamed up with and married Edna and they had two daughters. During WWII Pasey and Edna joined the USO, entertained the troops overseas, toured the country with the big band stage shows, and played the nightclub circuit. We had a standing backstage invitation when they were in town and were always star-struck when we met the headliners.

Although I was almost always ashamed to tell anyone my last name because of my mother's widespread notoriety, I was always anxious to brag about my famous show business uncle whose last name was also Winik.

I am so proud of my Uncle Pasey that I beg Ma for dance lessons. For a time, either Ma or Rowena shleps (takes, drags) me to the popular Rose Sidman's Dancing School in Roxbury where I dance happily, my imagination filled with dreams of fame and fortune. Each year, I eagerly practice for the dance recitals and never lose my enthusiasm for the opportunity to dance in front of an audience. At eight-years-old when I graduate to private tap lessons and start to prepare for another recital, Ma casually tells me she has cancelled the lessons because the dance teacher said that I am a klutz (clumsy) and can't learn the routines. I don't believe her reason for doing this, and am sure that the more likely explanation is that she doesn't want to pay for the lessons any more, and is tired of the hassle of taking me to Roxbury. What she apparently doesn't notice or care about is the cruelty of her

23

actions. She steals from me something I am passionate about and which gives me a sense of accomplishment. Today, a Broadway musical dance scene often summons in me that feeling of loss and deprivation.

Grandpa Sol died suddenly from a heart attack on the day after the bombing of Pearl Harbor, but Daddy, Becky and Mucky were able to keep the company going with government contracts to supply the area's military bases. After the war, however, the bases severely curtailed their operations and the business failed. Daddy was no longer the heir apparent to his parents' flourishing business. With little formal education and few employment options, Daddy and Becky were stymied as to what their next move should be. They knew they were lucky to be offered work in their uncle's meat trucking firm. Daddy was now just another meat-*schlepper* whose glory days were officially over.

Seven

Rowena, the cherished first-born grandchild of both our parents' families, had a pretty face, light hazel eyes, and a mop of thick dark brown hair. As a child, she looked like one of those chubby cherubs in an Italian Renaissance painting. As a teenager she was popular with her friends, endearing, unspoiled, and entirely without guile.

When Ma went out, she expected Rowena to *schlep* me around. My sister did this uncomplainingly, even when she planned to meet friends. If we were going to the movies, my requirement to take my *boulya-ba* (baby bottle) along pushed her close to the limit of tolerance. One bottle provided more than enough embarrassment for Rowena, but I always insisted on several. I would slug down one after another, happy that Daddy wasn't there to ration my milk supply as he did at home when I whined for more. Rowena had heard my plaintive bedtime chant many times; "I want some more milk, I want some more milk." So, when she was in charge of me, she accepted my excesses, understanding that it was not the milk I craved, but the ability of the bottle to slake a powerful psychological thirst.

I was so attached to my big sister that when elementary school let out and she didn't have other plans, I waited near her school, beaming widely in eager anticipation of our fun together. During those afternoons, we watched our favorite TV shows, including *The Big Payoff*, starring Bess Myerson—the first Jewish Miss America. I gladly provided ice cream goodies purchased with coins I had saved.

Top billing went to our occasional Saturday excursions. Rowena and I visited the zoo to see llamas, lions, birds, and spent hours lovingly gawking at the elephants.

When we stayed home, Rowena prepared and served tuna sandwiches and Campbell's tomato soup (*Mmmm...Mmmm good*), and her simple fare seemed as grand to me as luncheon offerings at Buckingham Palace. Rowena was my substitute mother—always there, always attuned to my needs, always patient and kind.

When I caused the toilet to overflow, she cleaned up the flood and benevolently turned down my zealously squirreled away savings of $1.37 that I offered her in thanks.

It was Rowena who took me to get my first bra. In doing so, she saved me the humiliation she herself had endured when Ma thoughtlessly threw her one of her own ill-fitting hand-me-downs to use as her first bra. It was hard to put a price on that kind of caring which went a long way towards bridging the black hole inside me.

Although outwardly calm and reasonable, Rowena was certainly not unscathed by our home life. She had been knocked about and exposed to things well beyond her age and understanding. In fact, she claims witness to the moment of my conception. During a family vacation, she was sleeping in the bed next to my parents and became aware that something bad had happened during their coupling in the bed next to hers. A failure of my parents' birth control method had infuriated my mother and Rowena witnessed her castigating our father for it and shouting, "I'd better not be pregnant!" Even at such a young age, Rowena was able to put this coital accident into context when I was born nine months later. Ma never even attempted to deny the story. Actually Ma told me, on more than one occasion, that she wanted to abort the pregnancy but was happy she didn't.

It was no surprise that the hard psychological knocks of our situation brought out troubled aspects of Rowena's behavior. She often flouted authority, following only those societal rules she chose to obey. The library across the street banned her for being unruly. It was a warm and welcoming place and would have provided enrichment and safety for me, if only I had allowed myself to participate in its offerings. Instead, by completely avoiding the place as a result of Rowena's banishment, I unnecessarily assumed the tarnish of another family member.

It is my first day of fifth grade. My teacher reads my name, realizes I am Rowena's sister, and asks me to stand up. She asks, "Well, Miss Winik, are you a carbon copy of your older sister?" I innocently ask her what she means, assuming that a compliment is coming. But she replies with a frosty edge to her voice, "Well, I am wondering if you will be as defiant and undisciplined as Rowena. I certainly hope not." Instantly, I feel the flush of shame and embarrassment at being singled out in this way.

What this teacher didn't know, and didn't take the time to learn, was that I aspired to be a model student, fought hard to overcome the stigma I bore, and struggled to prove that I did not deserve the automatic bad rap. The teacher's hostile question and her unwelcome comment left me wondering what could possibly be so distasteful about my beloved sister to justify such a destructive introduction to a classroom full of my peers.

Eight

I am alone in our apartment with Ma. Suddenly, the doorbell rings and rings. She rises from the couch, pushes the buzzer, and lets the visitors in through the front door. I hear their strong footsteps coming down the outside hall, and when they enter, I see that they are four burly uniformed cops—among them, my familiar school crossing guard. Once inside our apartment, their sheer size fills the living room as they settle down in a circle to talk with Ma. She orders me to go to my room so I won't hear the discussion. I go only as far as the door of my bedroom and huddle against the doorframe, listening intently to their deep voices. I can hear everything they say. One of the cops gets right down to business and says bluntly, "Knock it off May. We know you're turning tricks in here. We've gotten calls about you and we're not stupid. Your children need you, and we don't want to have to take action. The scandal and punishment would hurt more than just you. Besides, we like you. Why don't you just quit the business?" Ma's answering voice is even and unafraid. She admits nothing, makes no guilty concessions. Soon the cops are gone and I am confused and afraid, wondering what will happen next. Are the cops going to come again to arrest her and take her away from us?

I try to think how I can save her. The answer soon comes—in a child's magical solution—I will be a good little girl at all times, and never, ever do anything that will cause the cops to take my mommy away. Yes, that's it! Everyone, especially the crossing

28

guard cop will tell the others, how good I am and they won't take Ma away because they'll know that she is a wonderful mother and a good person!

If Ma's modus operandi changed after visits like this, it was never for long. She relocated her venue to deflect attention. Her friend was always eager for some extra cash in exchange for the use of her spare bedroom. While killing time waiting for Ma to finish with the john, I played with some pennies on the living room table. I knew why we were there—Ma was doing the same thing she did at home—but there I had places I could go until it was over. In this strange place, I felt vulnerable and out of sorts. Locations like these were the exception, and my mother always quickly reverted back to the familiar schedule of mornings at home with her customers from 7:30 – 11:30 and no need to share her earnings with a middleman.

Although Ma may have been the most conspicuous hooker in Mattapan, it turned out she did not have the exclusive franchise. She was part of a small network of housewives and mothers who also "entertained." They were well-dressed, relatively attractive women who got along well with one another. Some of them lived close by and had kids I knew.

People were drawn to Ma's vitality and spirit. Always fashionably dressed and glamorous, she was considered by some to be a look-alike for the 1940's movie actress, Joan Crawford. Ma knew it, and flaunted her enormous breasts and shapely legs—her major physical assets. She was an object of attention and desire of the neighborhood men and the envy—along with the inevitable enmity—of the neighborhood women.

She not only used her looks to maximum effect, but she also used her street smarts, intuition, and duplicity. I loved Ma and always wanted desperately to please her. And yet, from a very early age, I was perpetually enraged and frustrated by her behavior. She had her own agenda, and sadly, we knew we were not at the top of it.

Ma's morning schedule usually went like clockwork. If I was running late for school, my tardiness could result in an awkward shuffle past an impatient john in the narrow hallway. If I didn't look at the john maybe I would be invisible. Thus, I earned nearly perfect school attendance, having learned early that it was always better to avoid being home in the daytime. Sick days at home were no exception; they were a frowned upon inconvenience to both Ma and us. Whatever comfort Rowena and I gained in taking a sick day, we paid the high price of coping with Ma's trade.

Then there were the encounters when I wasn't so invisible.

Ma is on the phone when a man named Eddie rings the doorbell. She lets him in while continuing with her conversation. I am in the kitchen doing my favorite chore—removing the groceries from their brown carton and lovingly putting them away. Having food in the house makes me feel cared for, hence Ma loves me. And I love Ma even more, because as young as I am, I understand she is doing most of the providing. Daddy never asks me if I need anything. I am most certain that if I didn't have shoes, he would not notice or offer to buy me a pair. It is a painful lesson. Sensing that Eddie has come for what all the others come for, I try to make things more civilized and less awkward by opening up the corned beef wrapped in the shiny white deli paper and offering it to him. After all, Eddie has brought fresh eggs for our family. He takes a few slices off the top and gobbles the meat eagerly. Ma finishes her phone conversation and ushers him into our bathroom, closing the door behind them.

Eddie leaves and Ma comes into the kitchen shouting at me, "Corned beef is expensive! Why did you give it to him? Es iz nor phar di aignah mishpocheh (it's only for our own family)!" I beg Ma's forgiveness and tell myself ruefully how bad I am to give away things that she was working so hard to get for our family. I have failed to be a good girl, and to my guilty mind, Ma will just have to see even more men to make up for the loss. Maybe the eggs Eddie always brings are part of Ma's price for her services. I will never know, but in my childish way, I dub him Eddie the Egg Man, for lack of the more accurate title, Eddie the John.

In Ma's universe, it wasn't hard to discern the priorities. First on her list was her business. Second was her social life with her boyfriend—yes, she made a distinction among the johns, her boyfriends, and her husband. Her third priority was far more complicated. She had to continually juggle her other activities with the role of wife and mother. When she was home with us, we were thrilled. When she was feeling good and sensed our happiness, she sometimes elevated the evening to a celebration by ordering sundaes which were delivered from the corner drugstore.

Ma's territory ran up and down Blue Hill Avenue and included downtown Boston and the North Shore communities—Revere, Lynn, Swampscott, and Marblehead. Even our vacation spots were sprinkled with business opportunities! One of her clients, a respected neighborhood physician, was the father of Rowena's friend. Then there was the shoe salesman who invited Ma into the back room to help him find shoes in my size while I waited in the showroom. There was the theater ticket agent who could magically produce seats for Ma to a sold-out show, and the optometrist—the uncle of my close friend—who regularly examined more than Ma's eyes.

Rowena found that unwanted, unsought information about Ma's tricks could actually be empowering, and she kept shame at bay by knowing which other children were tainted by their fathers' associations with our mother. For instance, a glance over at her friend, the physician's son, always reminded her that his dad was one of Ma's regulars.

Ma kept her diaphragm in the bathroom medicine cabinet on the top shelf. It was obvious that Ma had or was planning to do business when the diaphragm was missing. This knowledge never failed to disarm me.

Rowena and I were both attuned to Ma's body language down to the number of breaths she took when she ran into a customer out in public. We could tell when her voice dropped to a lower register, she mumbled out of the side of her mouth, and her eyes widened. "When am I going to see you?" she said in that unmistakable low, intimate voice. These were not ordinary social encounters. We could see that our mother was hard at work.

In Ma's later years, Rowena periodically gave her money to help her out when business was waning. She began to notice that when she did so, Ma talked to her the way she talked to her tricks. She would hint at her desire for money by asking in that low, intimate mumble, "Am I going to see you today?" It was the same breathy voice she used with the johns! Never mind that Rowena was her adult daughter—it was all about the money.

Over the years, Rowena and I figured out categories for Ma's numerous clients. First were the bottom feeders—the nameless, faceless customers who were no more than foot traffic to us. Ma considered them the "take-their-money-and-run" clients. The second category included those who were part of our daily lives—family men, merchants, and shopkeepers. The third were those rare people who were elevated to the "Friends and Family" category.

Ma certainly didn't always keep her life as a hooker separate from us and made some appalling decisions. Uncle Bud was one of these. He fell into Ma's third category of tricks. I don't know why Ma wanted us to call him Uncle Bud, but she did, and we never crossed her, no matter what.

Uncle Bud was generous towards Ma and took her out for lobster dinners. After all, Ma always made certain that she got something valuable out of every man she had a relationship with. As a john, Uncle Bud naturally had to pay for her services, but in order to cross over the line into uncle status, he clearly felt the need to buy her dinners.

Ma and Uncle Bud invite us to accompany them for one of the coveted lobster dinners. She knows that he has a nasty habit of masturbating while driving his car or while sitting at the table, with his hand under a dinner napkin. Apparently, it doesn't bother her a bit that we are certain to witness this unfortunate display. And notice it we did! Afterwards, Rowena and I rant and rave about Uncle Bud's disgusting behavior, swearing never to be seen in his company again. Ma shrugs us off in her usual way. This kind of thing simply is not noteworthy to her; she is getting what she wants from Bud and that is what matters. It is a tossup as to which scavenger should be boiled: Ma, Bud or the lobster.

A few years went by, and our memory of Uncle Bud had more-or-less faded when Ma suddenly mentioned to Rowena that he needed help catching up on paperwork in his office. She asked Rowena to work once a week for him, and told her that Bud would just show her the work to be done and then leave the office. He would pay her $50 for each time she worked. This was a huge sum of money in the 1950s, and Ma was pleased with herself for negotiating such a profitable deal. As far as she was concerned, Bud was the hen who laid the golden eggs. To refuse our mother meant disappointing her, so Rowena—with great reluctance—tried to focus on the money.

Thus began a routine in which, once a week, Uncle Bud took Rowena to his office, showed her the work she was to do, and left. Several hours later, he would return to the office and take her home. Rowena wondered why there was so little work for her to do, and spent much of her idle time chatting with friends on Bud's office phone. But after five weeks of this, Rowena could no longer stand the numbing boredom of having so little to do, so she quit. Thirty-five years later, Ma casually told Rowena that before leaving the premises, Bud would hide in the storeroom, watch the teenager at work, and masturbate. Our mother knew no bounds.

Nine

Ma and Daddy were alternately each other's best friend and worst enemy, and she was definitely the sharpest thorn in his side. He heard the rumors, saw the expensive clothes she wore, and knew of the fancy places she went without him. But he had absolutely no idea how to deal with or control her.

Daddy believed strongly in Hammurabi's code, even though he was unaware that he was practicing, in a distorted manner, the ancient Babylonian's code of law. His "eye-for-an-eye, a tooth-for-a-tooth" attitude gave forth his parading a bevy of girlfriends and hookers in front of Ma. She did not, as a rule, parade men in front of him—although there were notable exceptions—but he knew a lot of what was going on and found justification for his own actions in his own brand of payback time.

It is a Sunday afternoon. Daddy tells us he is bringing home a friend named Joan to introduce her to Ma, Auntie, Auntie's husband Joe, and me. She is a hooker, is divorced, and has two daughters plus a steady boyfriend. (Just like Ma, except for the divorced part).While we wait for their arrival, we giggle as Ma pre-arranges a signal with Joe to indicate if he likes Joan's looks. They decide that Joe will tap his right foot if he likes her.

Daddy arrives with her. She is a pretty bleach-blond who is wearing a dressy strapless frock as daywear. We sit and wait for the signal from Joe. So now, instead of visiting Benson's Wild Animal Farm and looking at lions and tigers like any normal nine-year-old kid, I am staring—transfixed—at my Uncle's shoe, waiting for the sign. Finally, his shoe taps indicating that Joan is a hit! Joe's signal instantly elevates Joan to near-family member. It is all so civilized.

Perhaps most ironic was Daddy's close friendship with the woman who had introduced Ma to her profession. For many years, he was solicitous of her and particularly attentive to her daughter, whom he taught to drive. He also gave more attention to her than to either Rowena or me.

Daddy had been an angry man for a long time. He realized he was going nowhere while he was still young. Losing his father and the family business cost him a promising future that would have been handed to him. Already, with little incentive and even less ambition, he had been functioning poorly in the role of husband and father for as long as I could remember. Then, the gradual appearance of unaccustomed and unexplained luxuries in our home, along with Ma's increasingly busy social calendar, was making him suspicious and cranky.

Ma's growing reputation had become a hot topic on the gossip network. The details were the kind of shocking and salacious information that was seldom heard—or even imagined—in the conservative 50s when women were expected to function happily and narrowly as dutiful housewives. May didn't fit that stereotype in any way, and her sins were of the blockbuster variety. Public knowledge cruelly exposed Daddy's ineffectiveness as a provider—and worse, his perpetual status of cuckold.

I often heard him confronting her in a blind fury and repeating the stories he had heard about her. Ma coolly denied the allegations, but Daddy was only partially convinced that she was telling the truth. At the end of these confrontations, he generally stomped out of the house shouting that he was going to end the marriage. Each time, he went to stay at Mucky's house for a couple of days during which the couple heatedly exchanged angry phone calls. But by the third day, Daddy was usually home again and our lives continued as before, with Ma plying her trade.

Oddly enough, there was a characteristic tenderness between our parents that somehow transcended the serious issues that surfaced repeatedly in their marriage. I can still see the two of them sharing the couch, curled up at each end with their feet touching in the middle, as if nothing had ever happened between them to sour their affection. To my childish view, they always seemed like a matched pair—like salt and pepper shakers that should never be separated. Their brand of affection continued as long as they were both alive, despite the long list of sexual liaisons they both engaged in.

How strange it would have seemed to anyone from outside our family to hear Ma and Daddy discussing—like two best friends—remedies for the case of crabs that he picked up from a girlfriend. Or, when they were discussing their favored sexual preferences, hearing Ma casually ask, "Am I better in bed than Joan?" It was beyond strange. At some point, I simply stopped trying to figure out their relationship and simply accepted it as unknowable.

Ma was not threatened or enraged by Daddy's escapades the way he was by hers. In fact, they seemed to afford her a certain amount of amusement. Did his confessions and the obvious proof of the existence of girlfriends assuage some guilty feelings she harbored? Perhaps so, that is, if she actually experienced feelings of that sort. On a more practical note, Daddy's dalliances simply freed up time and gave Ma further justification for her transgressions. Thus was the basis for the toxic *pas de deux* my parents danced throughout their marriage.

Ten

Meat trucking was all Daddy knew, but the demands of that kind of work narrowed his life drastically. His day started at 2:00 a.m., and his daily delivery route took him through southern New England, to Cape Cod and back. When his day's work was done, he came home exhausted and went to bed before dark. There were some occasional joyous moments when he allowed us to ride in the back of the empty truck while it rattled through the streets of Boston. Rowena and I would brace ourselves in the cargo area, open the gates at the back of the truck, and make faces at the drivers behind us in the traffic. We loved it!

When I was seven, Daddy seriously injured his back, could no longer drive his delivery truck, and laid around in agony for months before his doctor admitted him to the hospital for extensive traction. This treatment was ultimately successful, but the doctor strongly advised Daddy to change his job in order to avoid further injury. Together, Daddy and Ma struggled to find a new direction for him. Then a friend suggested that he investigate going into the taxi business as a driver, and Daddy soon took a job with a local cab company. Because of his poor eyesight, he was assigned to the daylight hours, which conveniently allowed Ma to continue her morning schedule.

Being in the cab business rejuvenated Daddy emotionally for a time. He reveled in the freedom to go as far and
wide as his passengers required. And he enjoyed the
interactions with a whole new set of acquaintances—other
drivers and passengers alike. When he came home, Rowena
and I loved listening to him recount the fun he had giving
his out-of-town passengers an overview of Boston and its
history. Freely confessing to having limited historical
knowledge, he nevertheless thoroughly enjoyed
embellishing the facts.

"And Paul Revere was born right here in Mattapan on
Blue Hill Avenue. Look, there's the place, 1333."

Back in our apartment, he often laughed and said, "The
passengers never knew the difference. Anyway, they loved
the entertainment!"

Ma appreciated Daddy's enthusiasm for life as a taxi
driver. But he failed to translate that into enough take-home
money to suit her. She was convinced he spent more time
playing the local pinball machines than working the busiest
hours of the day. When his buddies were not cruising
around the city or waiting at a cab stand for a fare, they
often gathered at a neighborhood sundry store (equipped
with pinball machines) to relax, and Daddy usually joined
them. He was soon dubbed "King of the Pinball." It was
good-natured kidding to everyone but Ma. It triggered Ma's
nagging button. But her reprimands failed to change his
behavior or improve his productivity. She wanted him to
take advantage of the "rush hours" at the end of the day and
to stay out driving until there were no more fares to pick up.
He just wasn't motivated by hard work and hustling to
make a buck.

Ma wanted Daddy to provide for us; he thought she was
money-mad. He wanted Ma to be simpler in her tastes; she

thought he was nuts. She was convinced that his earnings would not have enough impact to ward off the hand-to-mouth existence she foresaw. They fought, he raged, she lied, he lived with the lies.

I silently listened to their bickering. I too, as part of the jury, waited to learn how much he had "booked" and bought into Ma's litany that he could work harder. Therefore I better understood Ma's motivation (rescuing us from poverty) for her own profession.

Their arguing produced a vitalizing solution. They decided that owning their own taxi would add to their social status and Daddy's overall incentive. Ma's savings provided the down payment and gave him a new opportunity to succeed. His part was to earn a living. Once again, he became excited about his work. But, surely, somewhere in his gut he knew that getting this new chance had little to do with his efforts and more to do with the profitability of our mother's little secret.

For me, it was the start of an early education in business. Taxi talk and more taxi talk: medallions, financing, shifts, repairs, garages, drivers, owners. That was the way it was with everything. Whatever went on in the house or was discussed, I was there.

Ma is out on Christmas Eve. As a precocious pre-teen, I neatly step into her nagging shoes when Daddy comes home early from work. I raise my voice and tell him, "Daddy, it's a holiday. There's more money to be made. Go back to work!" Uncharacteristically, he listens to me without anger and decides to comply. After a pause, he suddenly says, "You can keep the tips if you come with me." Instantly, I experience a whole new set of emotions, all because I am included in my father's life. I hop into the cab and Daddy restarts his shift. We spent the rest of the evening as partners, picking up and delivering customers — it is a delicious experience. At the core of my being, I sense that this must be what it feels like to be normal.

Despite that tender moment of togetherness, even I knew he was failing to hold up his end of the bargain.

Eleven

Ma bought my sister a small phonograph for her 16th birthday and Rowena was now bringing home rhythm and blues records—the music that was the rage among her black high school friends. She had me dancing around the house to Johnny Otis' *Gee Baby* and *Mambo Boogie*, the Clovers' hit song, *Don't You Know I Love You?*, and Lloyd Price's *Lawdy Miss Clawdy.* To the Jewish people we knew in 1952, this music seemed totally foreign—even a bit scary. But Ma and I readily warmed up to the irresistible tempo and the lyrics. Most young, white, Jewish girls did not relate to R&B, and they certainly did not frequent black clubs like the Hi Hat and Louie's Lounge in the South End. But Rowena began to do just that! At the same time, her behavioral problems— which were already well-documented in elementary school—began to accelerate dramatically. She resisted the teachers' authority and was often disruptive. Accustomed to having no real direction from either Ma or Daddy, Rowena thought of herself as an independent soul—not a troublemaker. Why should she have bowed to adult authority when she had been responsible for taking care of herself and me since she was seven-years-old?

The high school principal began calling Ma and Daddy regularly to summon them to meetings during which they discussed possible disciplinary measures for Rowena. Then, on one monumentally disastrous occasion, Daddy showed up at one of these meetings without Ma. When he was faced with something he couldn't handle, he always relied on sheer bravado to keep the trouble at bay. I do not know what the provocation was, but soon Daddy and the principal began to engage in hostile accusations and finger-pointing. Then the worst thing of all happened. They came to a thoughtless, shouted agreement that Rowena would immediately be permanently withdrawn from school.

It was an appalling decision that emerged from two out-of-control egos and a total disregard for the far-reaching impacts on the life of a troubled sixteen-year old. Simply stated, it altered Rowena's life and sense of self forever. Those two adults—who should have been dedicated to setting an appropriate path for a confused kid—elected instead to throw a bomb into the middle of her life. She was left critically injured and alone in the rubble.

Now that she had been barred from public school, Rowena started sleeping late and languishing around our apartment. Ma, with her laser-like focus on business and money, made it clear to Rowena that being rudderless and unemployed was unacceptable, especially when she had clients coming in during the day. And so my sister went out and got a factory job assembling parts at Raytheon in Newton and settled into a routine. Daddy drove her to work every morning, and Rowena took the bus home. Although I was still a young child of nine, I knew—with a great sense of foreboding—that her life, already full of unpleasantness and hardship, was in free fall.

For a while, she went out with her old school friends, but now she was regularly coming home several hours later than usual. She had learned from Ma how to make excuses, and at first it seemed that she got away with the made-up stories. However, it was happening too often, and each time the excuses became flimsier.

One day, Rowena came home and told Ma that she had discovered she was a lesbian. For Rowena, the newfound knowledge had come as a blessed relief—the most plausible explanation for why she had never felt comfortable with the usual high school dating activities of her friends. Her secret girlish crushes on female classmates had led her to suspect for a long time that there was something defective about her. But now, the absolute knowledge that there were other girls and women like her was transformative.

Given the unusual tolerance of things sexual in our household, and the expectation that in our family we always protected our own (as Ma had taught us so well), Rowena was justifiably taken aback at the explosive reaction she received. Learning of her new-found gay status was shocking enough for our parents, but Rowena further revealed that she had a 32-year-old girlfriend named Evelyn. Then, when it became clear that the girlfriend was black, Ma and Daddy came unglued. It was then that Rowena saw beyond a doubt that she was an exception to the family rule of *Protect Your Own, No Matter What*. What a terrible irony it was, that in a family with as many strange and twisted realities as ours had, this would be the only one our parents focused on as contemptible.

Wrath and passion were white-hot on both sides. Sometimes the three managed to engage in quiet discussion, but far more often, there were arguments and threats. Sometimes the lines blurred and Rowena could not tell if the brawls were about her sexual preference or her racial choice. Ma and Daddy demanded that Rowena stop "doing it." She insisted that being gay was not a "do" but an "is." She wondered aloud how it was that they had focused on her as the family scourge. What about intentional acts like old fashioned adultery and prostitution? Weren't those further up the list of activities that could send a person to Hell?

While all of this was going on, I remained quiet, contorted with pain, and thinking in my childish way that the member of our family to whom I looked most often for comfort and support—my rock, my sweet-natured sister— was now revealed to be as defective as the rest of us. I didn't know how else to process the information. Not a single soul ever took the time to explain any of this to me, so I was left to fashion my own theories and rationalizations. In the process, I simply shut down and began a long, lonely vigil, hoping for the end of this new nightmare.

Twelve

Other children were afraid of the dark, green monsters, the Soviets, the Cold War, or the bomb. We learned about the bomb at school and in movie theaters through short films touting the safety procedure "Duck and Cover" as an antidote to an atomic bomb attack. But unlike other children, I barely focused on such things. My concerns were instead concentrated on Ma and the possible fallout from her chosen profession.

When I was a child, I tried desperately to believe we were a normal family. I suppose my definition came largely from television shows like *Father Knows Best* and from glimpses of the families of friends. It seemed to me that other families did more together and lived more comfortably. They didn't have mothers who entertained strange men in their houses or fathers who spent most of their time at home lying on the couch. Still I maintained the self-delusion, that I could bring normalcy to my family. That notion permeated many childhood memories.

But one way or another, Ma sucked us all into a deviant world, and our lives were consumed by it. There was always an elephant in the room—a constant reminder of Ma's desire for a better material life for our family, and her willingness to do almost anything to get it. Even at the tender age of six, I had a rudimentary sense of morality, and I knew that my mother was breaking the rules. But my sister, Rowena, and I loved Ma unreservedly and let her influence overpower us in all matters. What could we do but go along? We were there to protect and serve her.

Each ring of the doorbell—especially those that fell outside Ma's stated office hours—sounded an alert that told me my sanctuary was about to be defiled. I might even have felt some jealousy because, when she opened the door to greet the invader, her attention was instantly diverted from any family contact or activities. Whatever amusement I had concocted for myself had to be put aside so I could make myself scarce. In addition, the low murmuring of the initial negotiation accompanied by the visitor's heavy breathing always made me feel nauseated. Trying to continue my play elsewhere in the house, I could never rid myself of the hyper vigilance the presence those men caused.

On evenings when we gathered as a family for a meal and maybe a TV show, a desperate john occasionally rang our doorbell at 8 or 9 p.m. looking for Ma's services. She would open the door and shout down the darkened hallway, "You rang the wrong bell!" Then Rowena and I would seamlessly slip into our accustomed enabling roles. "Yes," we agreed in a Greek chorus meant for our father's ears, "he must have meant to ring the Levins' doorbell." If Ma was out with her boyfriend, Rowena and I went to the door and delivered the same lines down the hallway that Ma always shouted. We had this act down pat. I was able to perform it mechanically. My cool nonchalant response was balanced by an intense repressed anxiety. My stomach roiled.

Throughout these charades, Daddy never got off the sofa where he was sprawled, and never made a move to answer the door. He would stir slightly, grunt, and ask who was there. When we lied to him, just as Ma always did, he asked no more questions. Was he, like us, playing a role Ma had taught him? His need to be wrapped in denial must have been part of whatever happened to him during his marriage. It seemed to me that he had somehow lost his way, most of the time forgetting how to be a husband and a father, and losing interest in anything he might once have cared about or strived for. I can only guess at the reasons, but certainly Ma's activities must have contributed to his decline.

Even at this early age, I knew that I would not be able to rely upon the adults in my life for guidance. I couldn't cry out "Ma, Ma" or "Daddy" if I needed help. Anything that would provide me direction as I grew up would have to come from within. Ma taught me not to expect or ask for anything from anybody so I wouldn't be disappointed.

I am in elementary school. Our teacher posts certificates on classroom bulletin boards to show which of us had undergone yearly dental examinations. Classrooms compete against one another to be the first to reach 100% participation. The winning classroom will get a gold star for every kid. I am at risk for being the only one in the fourth grade without the certificate because Ma and Daddy are petrified of dentists; they never go to them, and certainly never take us. So they find it amusing to hear me plead for a dental exam and blithely ignore my requests. My plea falls on deaf ears. I simply take things into my own hands. Remembering the name of a dentist, I make an appointment for myself and ride the streetcar from my house to his office where he gives me the exam. It was a done deal by the time the bill arrives for Ma to pay. My certificate is already safely posted with the rest of my class. I get what I want!

I was already transcending from my childhood and taking on adult-like burdens. Rowena, being six and a half years older than I, put us at too wide a gap as youngsters to have real conversations about our fate. We were not born with a mission statement and certainly didn't have to write a survival guide. We knew what we had to do. I pledged to stay tough and survive despite all the confusion.

Thirteen

Rowena, when you were so callously turned out of school and during all those fights about your being gay and your lover, I understood so little, but I felt the pain. Why did our parents make your life so hard? You protected and nurtured me—generous with yourself and never asking anything in return. And yet, because I was so young, I could do nothing for you when you needed help.

Life at home was becoming intolerable for Rowena and one day she called to say she was moving in with Evelyn and never coming home again. Only weeks before, we were dancing happily around the house to Rowena's fabulous R&B records. Now she had run away, bitterly betrayed and unhappy, and totally without prospects. Rowena, my only savior and protector, my friend, my mother substitute, had left our house, leaving all her belongings behind, to join what seemed to me to be a freak show. Once again, I felt the familiar throbbing beat of abandonment. I wanted her back!

Ma hired a private detective to find Rowena, taking me along to her initial meeting with him. To this day, the sight of that downtown Boston police building—where I silently witnessed that desultory dissection of my sister's activities, appearance, and whereabouts—triggers in me a flood of confused feelings.

Eventually, Rowena called home and agreed to meet Ma and Daddy in Boston. I clung to the desperate hope that she would somehow return to my world. The detective warned our parents that Rowena might have set up the meeting in order to get a chance to sneak home and get her clothes while they waited at the appointed location.

Daddy—in another show of ridiculous and terrifying bravado—made a plan to stake out our house and intercept Rowena if she returned while Ma was at the designated rendezvous site. His plan was to arm himself with a souvenir World War II machete—which had always been kept high up on a pantry shelf—and lie in wait for his firstborn daughter. I still wonder if he had any idea what he was going to do.

At the exact moment of the planned meeting, Daddy lay on the sofa holding the machete, lying in wait. Left with him in our dark, silent apartment, I trembled violently and prayed silently that my sister would not fall into this monstrous trap. I wondered, was he going to butcher Rowena or simply cut her in a few places just to show her who was boss! I desperately formulated a childish plan to signal Rowena to run back out the door the minute she arrived, and lurked silently in my bedroom doorway to carry out the plan if needed. But Rowena did not show up at either the rendezvous location or at home. She stood us all up!

Rowena was now part of the gay community, a thoroughly marginalized, vilified group of people in the 1950s. Her new friends, who had survived in that hostile world far longer than she, taught her how to live her life as a closeted gay person, telling her that living a lie was the only way to remain safe. Since she had already mastered the art of lying in our household, this was a logical progression for her.

Rowena suddenly surfaced again and asked Ma to meet with her at Evelyn's apartment in a neighborhood so rough that even the Boston Police were wary of going there. Ma made her own plans and took the cops with her to the address Rowena gave her. Evelyn was immediately arrested for harboring a minor. I saw Evelyn for the first time at Police Headquarters where I went with Ma after the arrest. If she had been Lena Horne herself, my emotional chaos would still not have abated at the sight of her. But dumpy and ugly Evelyn was no Lena Horne. She was handcuffed while being led to a holding cell where she was to stay for the weekend. Rowena was sent to the Convent of the Good Shepherd in Boston and a court hearing was scheduled for Monday morning.

Ma had exposed us to many things far beyond our understanding and sophistication, but Rowena's detention in a Catholic convent was a new one on all of us. We were Jewish people living in the center of an intensely Jewish community. We had often been warned not to cross Norfolk Street because that was where the Gentiles lived, and we had been told they would beat up any Jews found in their territory. Jails we knew about from the movies we went to on Saturday afternoons. What did we know about a convent?

At the hearing that followed, Evelyn was convicted of "Contributing to the Delinquency of a Minor" and was sentenced to two and a half years at the Framingham Correctional Institution. Rowena was declared a "Stubborn Child" and ordered to submit to a ten-day inpatient observation at Boston Psychopathic Hospital. Hearing all this, I was filled with terror. What would they do to my sister in such a place? Rowena had not committed any crime nor was she crazy. But clearly, the homophobic legal system had no idea what else to do with her. (It wasn't until the pivotal Stonewall riots in 1969 when the police raided a gay bar in Greenwich Village and the patrons fought back, that the gay community began to galvanize itself.)

I wondered what Evelyn would do to us when she was released and was beside myself with fear that she would come back and kill us all for sending her to jail. At that point, I could more appropriately be classified as a mental patient than Rowena.

Now, at nine years old, I felt completely abandoned. After losing my ally so abruptly, my life had become surreal. Police, machetes, a black woman girlfriend, dykes, jail sentences, lies and more lies, courtrooms, convents, and mental institutions — these were the problems that began to cohabit with the familiar demons my home already harbored in abundance.

Ma experienced some rudimentary feelings of self-reproach. She assumed, along with many others in that socially unenlightened period of the 1950s, that Rowena's sexual preference was a direct result of our mother's lifestyle. Ma didn't like to feel guilty about anything, so she visited the hospital every day, and spent a good deal of time explaining to Rowena how much she loved Daddy and how much she regretted that Rowena had believed otherwise. I can only assume that she thought her behavior had "turned" Rowena into the caricature of a man-hating lesbian. Ma knew that Rowena was terrified; but after unburdening herself in this rather perfunctory and laughable manner, Ma was ready to have some fun. She started accompanying Rowena to the daily therapeutic activities at the hospital. The two of them had a lot of laughs at the psychodrama sessions, and she had served as Rowena's willing dance partner at the afternoon socials. For years after, Ma treasured the potholder the two of them made together at occupational therapy. There were times when I thought of that lowly potholder as a visible symbol of the raw emotion affecting us all during such an uncertain time in our lives. I do believe that Ma suffered during this time, and worried that my sister's life would never be easy or normal.

After the hospital observation phase, the court mandated that Rowena see a psychiatrist weekly for a minimal cost. In all, this was a positive thing, because it opened up an avenue that would allow her to explore her troubles from early childhood into adulthood. Ironically, many years later, my first full-time job as a nurse was at Massachusetts Mental Health Center—formerly the Boston Psychopathic Hospital. The despair about Rowena's situation, which I had sublimated for so many years, drew me to that assignment. I needed to understand what it had been like for Rowena in that place. It was an unsettling experience—and in the face of every patient I cared for, I saw the reflection of my brokenhearted sister's gentle, young face.

Fourteen

As an emerging ten-year-old, I began to deliver lippy, judgmental statements to my mother in crude attempts to reform her. I fantasized that these efforts would have the effect of waving a magic wand over Ma and turning her into a normal, housewifely, child-centered mother.

One day, after Ma's trick leaves, I deliver the lines I have practiced over and over in my head. They are designed to instantly chastise and reform her. "Ma, I hate you and all the men that come here. You are disgusting. Why can't you be like other moms who don't do what you do? I wish you weren't my mother!"

Upon hearing my outburst, Ma immediately explodes in a fury, "You ungrateful, little bitch." I leap for the door and run up Blue Hill Avenue past the Chinese laundry. I hear her pounding the pavement behind me, breathing heavily while yelling about my chutzpah (nerve). "You brat. Stop. I said STOP!!" I pass the Texaco station. I run faster—it seems I am running for my life.

I turn off the sidewalk and dash up a hill overgrown with weeds. Maybe I can hide. The weeds reach to my neck. The thick growth instantly slows my progress, and Ma is able to grab me from behind and bring me down. She shrieks in my face, slaps me painfully, and tries to catch her breath. "How dare you challenge me? Who are you to say that to your mother? Answer me. How dare you! I said, Answer Me!"

I wait for the final blow. Just as suddenly as this drama starts, Ma takes a few deep breaths and visibly begins to calm down, while she picks the weeds off our sweaty faces. Weeping, I cover my throbbing face and after a long pause, she says to me — "How about I buy you an ice cream?"

Could it be that Ma is sorry for what she has just done? Does she somehow realize my pain? Does she understand that my powerful love for her has driven me to such cheekiness? Whatever the reason, we are now far from home, and I sense we are both equally miserable about what has just taken place. This time, I do not feel guilty or sorry for my behavior. If anything, I am hopeful that Ma's guilt about losing her temper in this manner might somehow lead to her miraculous conversion. I stop crying, and start smiling, "Sure, Ma. I want a hot fudge sundae. What are you getting?"

"Me, too," she replies, and together we walk, her arm around me, toward the ice cream parlor. The heat of the moment is completely spent!

Fifteen

There were times when Ma turned our cramped apartment into a festive party room and enjoyed inviting Daddy's taxi buddies, their wives, and some of our family members to her Jewish holiday turkey dinners. Other times, she threw a party for no particular occasion. Ma loved to entertain company. Uncle Pasey, the perennial Peter Pan, was often included because he exuded the show business glitz we loved. Daddy animatedly participated with everyone. He seemed to have endless energy for others, but when he was alone with us, he just seemed to turn off. It was painful.

Because Rowena was older, she remembers that her childhood with Daddy was more conventional and positive than mine. He would relate tales from the *Arabian Nights* and together, father and daughter enjoyed the adventures of the *Knights of the Round Table*. Such was her childlike love for Daddy that Rowena was not surprised that the king was named Arthur—our father's given name. Rowena and Daddy were also bonded together in their love of baseball. Even as a toddler, she stayed up nights with him listening to Red Sox baseball games on the radio. By the age of eight, she knew all the baseball line-ups as well as he did.

I was innocent enough to believe I could change Daddy into the kind of father I saw in the community. I begged him to take us on Sunday family outings and brought home brochures describing local points of interest to entice him. Sure, I was a little kid dying to be taken to the wild animal farm, but for me the begging was not really about seeing monkeys and elephants. I simply longed for my family to be typical and wholesome. To my childish mind, if we all went there together, we had a shot at being a normal family.

The opportunities for fun with him became so infrequent that I began to invent ways to initiate it. Since he was an avid fan of slapstick, I decided one day to prank him by dousing him with a full glass of water while he was lying on the couch. He loved it! From then on, my occasional surprise water attacks were a perpetual winner for me and never failed to give us something to laugh about together.

Although Daddy made only a minimal parental investment in us, he was easily insulted if he thought we were disrespectful in his role as patriarch. He often lectured us about what good parents he and Ma were because they did not drink. This claim would then be closely followed with his pledge that if we were sick and/or needed blood, we could count on him. That strange assurance meant to me that we had to be ill or bleeding in order to get his attention. And despite his claims to the contrary, out of the three times I was hospitalized, Daddy showed up only once. The one time Rowena was in the hospital, he didn't show up at all.

I never could predict what would make Daddy enthusiastic. So, when I ran for treasurer in the 9th grade, I was completely amazed when he suddenly appointed himself my campaign manager and speechwriter. Ma was not at home—possibly on a trip with a boyfriend—and he and Rowena designed VOTE FOR DALE WINIK posters for me to hang on the school walls. When I won the election, Daddy seemed prouder than I was. This rare instance of support made me very happy!

"Daddy, what happened to you?" I sadly asked myself throughout the years. A broken soul, your life seemed so limited. Pictures of you, in your 20's and early 30's, playing cards with your friends or in your spiffy riding habit didn't reflect the same man I knew growing up.

At some point, Daddy seemed to no longer take any pride in his appearance. He began to look *schlumpy* (slovenly). He stopped showering, stopped changing into clean clothes with any regularity, and never brushed his teeth. The bad breath and body odor I associate with my father lingers in my olfactory memory even now. I am certain he never would have changed his clothes if Ma did not put clean ones out. He had to be cajoled into taking even an occasional bath. As a general rule, he spent most of his time off enveloped in the darkness of our apartment, either lying in the bedroom or stretched out on our living room sofa. He slept or watched TV, smoked Camels by the dozens, and occasionally sent us to the corner store to buy comic books or newspapers for him. Because of the near-certainty of his presence, Rowena and I seldom brought home friends if we could avoid it. He was an embarrassment to us.

Daddy never bothered to lift the toilet seat and often just peed on the seat and the floor. He rarely bothered to flush when he was through. When I used the bathroom after him, the yellow stains and the odor of urine triggered an intense nausea in me. I often scrubbed the toilet seat and floor with a vengeance until my fury and indignation subsided. He developed blackheads on his face and body and I sometimes mustered the courage to beg him to let me squeeze them—an activity now more politely referred to as a facial. It was a child's attempt to make her father minimally presentable and thereby single-handedly reshape her family's aberrant existence.

I believe it was his lack of respect for himself and his family that contributed strongly to the distance that steadily grew between Daddy and me. I wondered what his friends saw in my father beyond the blackheads and bad breath that revolted and shamed me.

Overall, he seemed to be a *shlimazel* (bad luck guy). He had very little interest in me, despite my best efforts to entice him into doing things that other fathers did with their children. Was it laziness, anger, or depression that made him this way? Probably all three, but as a child I certainly didn't understand the complexities of the human psyche and was simply in search of an occasional show of attention. His consistent indifference had the effect of raising Ma's status higher and higher, until she was *the* parent—no longer one of two. I exclusively looked for whatever small comforts I could pry out of her. In return for her largesse— with Ma, everything had to have some return—I was pledged to protect her, even when doing so involved using lying and manipulation against her own husband. With such unchallenged authority, Ma was free to follow her own selfish pursuits, knowing that her adoring fans would accept whatever crumbs she scattered.

I am talking on the telephone to a friend. Daddy yells from the other room, "Hang up! You've been on too long!" I keep talking, taking my time to finish the conversation. Suddenly Daddy charges into my bedroom in a blind rage. With his belt in hand he beats me until I have cuts and welts all over my body. Ma can't calm him down or pull him off me, and Rowena is not there to protect me, so I am a sitting duck for his unrestrained rage.

I cannot finish the school week because of my unsightly and painful injuries. Ma's solution to the problem is to get a separate phone line installed specifically for the kids' use. It is this incident more than any other that helps me to understand that I long ago emotionally separated myself from my father. In spite of the palpable soreness of my body, I feel no worse than any other normal day in his presence.

To this day, when I observe loving fathers interacting with their kids, it evokes a deep melancholy within me as I realize once again how much Daddy and I both missed. And when I see my son acting as a loving father to his children, I realize that I really never learned as a child that the relationship between father and child could be so natural, easy, and mutually satisfying.

Sixteen

For many years, when Ma's business day ended, she had a standing date. She had found a way not only to survive, but to thrive, and now had increased income plus a lively outside social life. Ma spent afternoons with Eddie, her married boyfriend, and did not take kindly to any disruption of her stolen time with him. It was painfully obvious that she resented it when one of us was ill and had to stay at home. Inevitably she'd ask the malingerer, "Do you care if I go out?" We could have been dying, but we knew enough to answer, "No, Ma."

I think Ma saw her life with Eddie as her real life— because it was the one that made her feel truly alive. With Eddie, she believed she was living to the hilt. He was a salesman and maintained his own appointment schedule. This allowed him the flexibility that Ma needed. They had lunch together, saw movies, and shared good times with a group of cronies. They went clubbing at least one night a week and were known within their circle as fabulous dancers.

Rowena and I were frequently woven into their plans and, oddly, we both benefited from the relationship. Eddie was a kid's delight; he took us to amusement parks, to movies, to the beach and to New York City. There, he took us to a Chinese restaurant where we had pork strips in wine sauce, the kind of exotic treat which we eagerly anticipated on such trips. On the way home, he would stop at a special candy store where he bought us white chocolate—a new phenomenon in those days. On other occasions, Ma and Eddie took me to New York's Roosevelt Hotel and danced the evening away to Guy Lombardo and his orchestra. I sat at the table and watched!

Eddie noticed us, played with us, and sometimes even disciplined us—the way a father might. One day while at the movies with them, he did not let me eat all the candy I wanted, so my wild-child war cry became "Eddie Is a Jerk." The shortened version of this impertinence—EIJ—immediately became his official nickname. He could be a warm, affectionate man, and comfortably filled the void left by our apathetic and uninvolved father. We loved him for it.

Rowena and I were not only amused by the Ma-EIJ relationship—we were also used and abused by it. When Ma needed to explain her countless evening absences with EIJ to Daddy, she wrapped her alibis around Rowena and me. We wove larger and larger lies to hold off our father's suspicions.

Daddy: Where were you?

Dale/Rowena: At the movies.

Daddy: What did you see?

Dale/Rowena: The new William Holden movie.

Daddy: Why are you home so late?

Dale/Rowena: We watched it twice.

He soon abandoned the questions to preserve his sanity, his dignity, or both. We dreaded these inquisitions because they made us feel bad and further estranged us from him.

He must have known he could try harder to catch us in the lies, but opted instead to save face.

Bubbe often went to the movies on Friday nights, and Ma, instead of taking me to the clubs, asked her to take me along to the movie. This was a relief to me. After the movie, Bubbe invariably took me to the corner drugstore where we sat on counter stools and ate yummy sundaes from silver cylinder holders lined with white paper cups. My selection was always vanilla ice cream with hot fudge and marshmallow topping, and she always had chocolate with pineapple sauce on top. But after our mutual treat, the tension mounted while we waited at Bubbe's for Ma to pick me up. My grandmother complained bitterly when Ma was late, and I always felt uncomfortable and unloved when I saw how out of sorts my presence had made her despite the otherwise pleasant evening we had spent together.

Other times, Ma left me with her favorite cousin while she and EIJ went on the town. I played with the cousin's children until bedtime. Then, I would sit in the den with the adults—thoroughly chagrined—as we all pretended we were not exhausted while silently counting the ticks on the clock until Ma came through the door to take me home.

Sometimes, Ma dropped me off alone at the movies to watch a show while she went out.

And there were many evenings—at the Latin Quarter, the Mayfair, the Frolics, or some other chic Boston nightclub—when Ma and EIJ danced together for what seemed to be hours while I nodded off at the table. The only value my presence brought was the alibi it provided. I was always the only child in the club, unless Rowena was also there. I was keenly aware of the other patron's disapproving stares and imagined their children were safely tucked away at home.

I am assigned to act as look-out to watch for cops from the back seat of the car while Ma and EIJ conduct steamy sex in the front. Near total meltdown, revolted by the unwelcome sights and sounds emanating from the front seat, I am terrified that if I close my eyes for even a moment, the cops will storm the car by surprise and drag Ma and EIJ away, leaving me alone and vulnerable to any number of unspeakable terrors.

I still have not been able to obliterate from memory the sight of EIJ entering Ma from behind while she stared out the car window into some middle distance bathed in moonlight.

Ma and EIJ's relationship could often be a mudslinging and volatile affair—mainly because he hated the fact that she was a hooker. So, when I was twelve, she finally tired of his frequent verbal onslaughts and terminated their longstanding relationship. No one got between Ma and her profession and still remained a part of our family circle.

EIJ had been a part of my life since I was six months old and his departure set me adrift emotionally. I was completely heartbroken. When he did not stay in touch with me, I wondered, "Doesn't he love me like a daughter?" His abandonment ignited my growing sense that I was somehow unworthy.

Another key player in Ma's life was Auntie. She was Ma's best friend as well as her "child." Auntie's life, with all of its ups and downs, became part of our daily living. She was stolid and inane, often seeming insensitive to her environment and the people around her. Sometime during the EIJ period—perhaps when I was about eight—Auntie married a man named Joe and they had a son, Dennis. A year later, the couple divorced and Joe was thrown in jail for non-support. When this happened, the ever-vigilant, ever-controlling Bubbe ordered Ma to augment Auntie's income so that she could live in a decent place near us. There was no argument. When we ate, Auntie and Dennis ate. When we slept, Auntie and Dennis slept. When we went on summer vacations to Revere Beach, Ma paid for a room for Auntie and Dennis. I became Dennis' designated babysitter so that Ma and Auntie had plenty of unrestricted time together. I didn't mind spending so much time with Dennis; he was a lovable little boy, and provided good company for me in the many hours when I might have otherwise been alone. Besides, who better than I could teach him the rules of the road concerning the Mish triumvirate?

After Auntie's divorce, Ma fixed her up with Bob, a single guy she knew in the neighborhood. The two eventually married and Bob adopted Dennis. Shortly after, their only child, Freddie, was born. Ma never let anybody forget she had created that neat little package for Auntie. But Bob soon introduced an unexpected wrinkle; he did not want to deal with Ma's sullied reputation, so he no longer allowed Auntie to see her. Both sisters were surprised and devastated, but Auntie was too scared to flee from the security that Bob offered. Ma was torn between rage and understanding and often vented her feelings to us. Auntie toed the mark for a while, but little-by-little, her need to see Ma overcame the fear of disobeying Bob's mandate. They began meeting each other—at first on a clandestine basis— then more openly. Now, like Ma, Auntie was living in two separate worlds.

Seventeen

Ma always said: "If I can't be rich, I want to be where rich people are." In the early 1950s, Ma took Rowena, Auntie, and me on the first of our many Florida vacations. This was a pilgrimage well-suited to Ma's hunger for glitz and fast living and was destined to become an annual event. Consistent with Ma's priorities, she never stinted on fun if she could help it, so she made plans for us to be there for the entire month of February. Our schools were reluctant to put the stamp of approval on a month's absence and made Ma pledge to keep us on a study plan they laid out. That quickly taken care of, Ma was eager to get started on our adventure.

In those days, Miami Beach was rapidly becoming a winter Mecca for wealthy New Yorkers plus others who could afford to take advantage of the increasing availability of air travel. This was considered a luxury and people dressed up for it. We boarded in grand style, Ma wearing her mink stole and gloves, Auntie similarly attired, and Rowena and I dolled up in our finest, following Ma like two excited ducklings.

When our plane flew directly into a lightning storm over Florida, the majority of the passengers traded in their lunch boxes for airsick bags while Rowena and I calmly ate the egg salad sandwiches we scavenged from these no-longer-hungry fellow passengers. Because of the ferocity of the storm, our plane was forced to land in Jacksonville. Clearly more disturbed by this incident than we were, Ma vowed that any subsequent trips to Miami would be in cars, trains, and/or buses. She kept to this vow for many years thereafter.

Once in Miami, Ma talked the talk of the posh ocean side hotels north of Lincoln Road, but in actuality, the four of us walked the walk at the modest Metropole Hotel, south of Lincoln Road. This was the area that would later evolve into the trendy South Beach. We loved the Metropole because we got to know the regular patrons and thoroughly enjoyed the traveling entertainers who performed weekly in the hotel's intimate lobby. Ma knew who she was and what she needed—she knew there would be no singing of Yiddish songs in the lobby of the fabulous Saxony.

We visit the most impressive hotels in Miami and dine out with a cadre of Ma's men friends from New York. News of her activities quickly finds its way to Boston and straight into Daddy's burning ears. She learns that he had risen from his couch with the intention to drive from Boston to Florida to confront her about the gossip. She is actually frightened. (This is a first, as far as Rowena and I could tell.) Ma's fear is co-mingled with a large dose of pure resentment. The last thing she wants is for her husband to intrude upon her private Utopia.

Rowena and I begin a three day vigil. Daddy finally arrives and is exhausted from the long drive, but begins the accusations and fighting as soon as he walks through the door. Our parents scream, yell, and trade recriminations at a high decibel level. Rowena and I cling together and imagine the worst things that might happen. After two hours of intense fighting, they emerge from the room as if there had never been a problem or a crisis. Ma works her wiles on Daddy and convinces him to spend the rest of the month with us. Daddy is Ma's loyal codependent, and as always, he simply rolls with the punches.

In the end, what did it matter that he had felt the need to drive all the way to Florida to have it out with his errant wife. He was compliant now, and our family was still intact.

"Normal" families have boxes and albums full of important memories. They consist of pictures of babies, birthday parties, picnics, family pets, childhood firsts, grade school pictures, and any number of familiar themes featuring their children. Our family was different. Our boxes contained dozens and dozens of pictures of Ma and Auntie—posing with a large and revolving cast of characters including a chimpanzee wearing a Florida tee-shirt and jogging shorts, numerous men whose names I have long ago forgotten, and occasionally, Daddy. The sisters were photographed at nightclubs, hotel bars, on shipboard dressed in gaudy cruise wear, on hotel verandas, lying next to swimming pools, dancing to a cabaret band, and standing in the water glamorously posing as if waterskiing. There is even a picture of Bubbe looking like a painted wooden nutcracker figure, with her aging face, her low square jaw, and long, pencil-thin mouth, frozen in a half smile. She is posing in a cardboard boat labeled "Miami Beach" and balanced on hand-painted, stylized waves. Yes, sir, this was the life! We were welcome to come along on Ma's adventures if we wanted, but we knew not to complain or demand anything. This was Ma's show and she had earned it.

Never was this last point clearer to me than when I went to Florida with Ma and a guy named Sam, a blue collar working man from Watertown.

Sam and Ma are in front of Filene's downtown department store near the famous clocks. They eye one another. Ma thinks he is the cutest thing she has ever seen. Naturally, they get together for a brief fling. Ma talks appreciatively and expansively about the athletic sex they have, and decides a trip to Florida with Sam will be fun. She invites me to go along—probably as an alibi. I am fourteen and desperately want to believe Ma values my company. We all stay in one room together—Ma is cheap that way—and the two of them keep very busy screwing in the next bed. I am furious at myself because I should have known this would happen, but did not have the strength to resist the desire to be with my mother. Finally, I blurt, "Ma, I can't take this; I'm not staying here anymore." I hope she might change the arrangements or use more discretion.

But she says, "Good, go home." And so I go home—alone. I suspect she is delighted to finally be alone with Sam.

There was not a lonelier feeling for a teenager than to experience her beloved parent simply not caring if she stays or goes. That's the way it went with Ma. She was a charismatic figure, and Rowena and I—and most certainly, Daddy—wanted to bask in her life-giving rays. But we always flew too close and got our wings melted. When we pushed back and tried to protect ourselves, she offered no resistance, no clue that she even cared. That cool, unemotional, "Good, go home," was just one of the many ways she let her family know exactly where we stood.

Eighteen

Florida wasn't our only regular vacation escape. When I was seven, Ma started a practice of relocating our family to a hotel at Revere Beach as soon as school ended each year. The hotel was a wooden firetrap which accommodated 40 to 50 families in small one-room quarters with paper-thin walls and no bathroom facilities. Each family slept, cooked and ate in that one room and co-existed with swarms of ever-present flies. There was little privacy, and we all shared the sounds of our neighbors' laughing, squabbling, nagging, lovemaking, and snoring. As if that were not enough, the enforced camaraderie was pushed to the limits by the necessity to queue up for use of the outdoor toilets and showers.

On rainy days we congregated in the simple lobby where the adults gossiped and the kids indulged in day-long marathons of Monopoly and Canasta. Hot nights made the rooms stuffy and unbearable, and we often took our blankets across the street to the crescent-shaped stretch of sand along the Atlantic Ocean in search of a better night's sleep. With the discomfort and lack of privacy we all endured living in such an arrangement, it seemed a miracle that each year, as Labor Day approached, families quickly reserved their one-room getaways for the next summer. We cried while saying our mutual goodbyes.

Bubbe and Auntie always stayed at the beach too. Their presence offered a special opportunity for me—time with Bubbe's third husband, Moishe, who commuted daily to his work at a dry cleaning plant in Boston and returned to the hotel at night. He spoke only Yiddish, but kept me company and filled the emptiness on countless summer evenings when the other adults in our entourage were busy with their own interests. Next to the hotel was Roger's Pizza and occasionally I would help the owner cut up the pizzas in exchange for free day-old, warmed-up pizza. Basically, this activity filled some of my idle hours and I enjoyed eating the rewards, but I counted on Moishe to keep me company a couple of times a week when I would otherwise have been alone or babysitting for Dennis.

Moishe was a free spirit with a sweet soul who made me feel warm and loved. He always had a cigar in this mouth, a ready smile, and walked like Charlie Chaplin's Little Tramp. He could afford only a modest lifestyle, and Bubbe complained about him unmercifully, but he was blessed with the gift of humor and tolerated her attacks with grace. She cruelly pointed out to all of us that he was the only *shtick drek* (low-class loser) in his otherwise elegant, somewhat wealthy family. When they were at home, she ordered him to smoke his cigars outside the house and sent him to the local gas station to use the toilet, explaining to us, "He's a *shtinkerer*." Rowena and I were aware of her obsession over control of the toilet. We felt bad about the way she treated good-natured Moishe. It was disconcerting, but I eventually considered her mean comments about her husband to be some sort of blustering, because they seemed to be together most of the time, and apparently got along well.

Moishe's weakness was his inveterate gambling. He played cards and bet on the numbers, horse and dog racing, and anything else he could find. Naturally, Bubbe was not at all tolerant about this vice. But when he took me to the arcades and gamely tried to win prizes for me, I loved him for it. He tossed balls, pitched hoops, and shot water pistols. I didn't care what the loot was—boxes of candy, knickknacks, dishes, goldfish, stuffed animals, Kewpie dolls, or live parakeets—whatever. As far as I was concerned, the things he won for me simply increased his superhero status. I felt some guilt when he spent the money because I knew Bubbe was sure to reprimand him, but I also knew he would be doing these things with or without me.

In addition to all the exciting bounty Moishe provided, he was jolly, mischievous, and—most important—he was *there* for me; a godsend. Even Ma, with her abiding toughness, had to concede that he was good to her and Auntie and performed like a father to them. This was extremely high praise from her. My younger cousin, Dennis, who eventually unseated me as Moishe's special grandchild, still remembers him as fondly as I do.

I had become inured to a lot of Ma's behavior. However, when our beloved Moishe died years later in Florida, Bubbe, Auntie, and Ma broke all their own disgraceful precedents. The way they talked, it was as though he had never been part of our family, to say nothing of the fact that he had been Bubbe's devoted husband for over thirty years. He could have been a total stranger for all the love and care they showed his memory!

This unholy trinity simply had no emotional mechanism for dealing with death. Not wanting to take any responsibility for funeral arrangements, they talked about contacting his children, whom he had not seen or spoken to in ages, and letting them handle it. It is still unclear to me what became of his remains, but, whatever happened, I am certain it was not the "right" thing.

Moishe's simple vices in the arcades and betting venues seem utterly benign compared to the questionable games my mother sucked me into—shoplifting and skipping out on restaurant checks. For these activities, her motto was, "buy one and steal more." One of the first instances I observed of Ma's callous disregard for the law was when she and Auntie boldly carried a coffee table from a store, eerily confident that no one would suspect they hadn't paid for it. They were right; no one did.

Ma and I are in Zayre's department store. She slips a bra into her pocketbook. However she isn't quick enough for the store detective who apprehends us at the door. Trembling and frozen to the spot, I wet my pants in fear of what might happen to us next. Fortunately he tells her he won't arrest her this time.

In today's more vigilant society, I might have been removed from my home and placed under child protection services.

Ma loved to eat in trendy restaurants, and especially enjoyed beating the checks. She trained Rowena and me to leave the restaurant immediately when we finished our meal with her. Her game was to stay behind and interact socially with the cashier so that casual observers assumed she was paying the bill. Actually, she was only buying a package of gum or getting change in order to deflect any suspicion. If the practice was for the wait staff to collect payment directly, Ma simply picked up the check, headed towards the ladies' room, and silently ducked out of the place with the unpaid check still in her pocketbook. I lost count of the times I waited outside a restaurant sweating and shaking with anxiety because of what Ma was doing inside.

Ma, Auntie, baby Dennis, Rowena and I are enjoying the corned beef sandwiches and potato pancakes at a popular deli in Newton. After our dessert, Ma instructs us to pull the car in front. Rowena is at the wheel. We wait. Soon Ma exits the restaurant and nonchalantly gets in. As we roar away, the manager comes screaming out of the restaurant after us. It is a scene from "Bonnie and Clyde"—without the guns. Ma seems untouched by the excitement, is thoroughly disgusted with my hysterical reaction, and hisses at me to stop acting like a baby. Rowena, long since inured to Ma's adventures in crime, finds a measure of excitement and, although she does not yet have a driver's license, frequently serves as our getaway driver.

And then there was the time when I saw her walk by a recently-vacated table and snatch the tip. It wasn't just the establishment she was willing to cheat; she ripped off the hardworking help as well. I don't know what kind of compulsion made her steal, but it was ever-present, and Ma never seemed to want to rein it in. She often paid for one thing and then dispassionately stole much more than the amount of the purchase.

When we were in Revere Beach one summer, she got a job at a local cafeteria as cashier. The casual grey dress she purposely chose to wear for the job had very large pockets with white trim. When she rang in a sale one dollar went into the register, and two went into her pocket. Ma apparently hadn't really thought out this scam very carefully, because within a few days, the management caught her red-handed and fired her on the spot.

76

As I grew into my teens, I stood by helplessly in the dressing rooms of some of the city's best stores watching Ma's illicit clothing acquisitions. In one unforgettable afternoon, Ma took my friend Myra and me shopping for dresses for my engagement party. Myra could not afford a dress she particularly liked so she bought a less expensive outfit. But when we returned to our car, Ma reached into her bag and triumphantly presented Myra with the expensive dress—she had boosted it. This made Myra and me both cry—but for entirely different reasons.

Beautiful clothes had long been a high priority for Ma. If she couldn't shoplift what she wanted, she maxed out her charge accounts at all her favorite stores. After she had completely destroyed her own credit, she started to feed off Rowena's hard-won credit, without my sister's knowledge. If she had to forge Rowena's signature to get what she wanted, so be it. Ma had already inflicted enough psychological damage on Rowena to keep her busy for years, but now, she had to slowly repair her personal financial status that Ma had ruined.

Rowena and I are shopping in the boutique Boston department store, Conrad and Chandler's. We are recognized from previous outings with Ma and the sales staff summons the store manager who races to the retail floor where she corners and pressures us to force Ma to pay her delinquent balance which by now was in the thousands of dollars. Then she escorts us out of the store. Unfortunately for her, she wrongly assumes that we have the power to influence our mother. But we both know that Ma has no conscience and will never pay her bill.

I liked good food and stylish clothing, but the pleasure of these things paled when they became evidence of Ma's criminal instincts. I always knew what she was up to. Should I have stamped my feet or waved my arms in the restaurant and dressing rooms to call attention to my mother's crimes while they were in progress? Should I have screamed in her face as I had as a very young child while trying to drive away her tricks? Should I have run away from her? Perhaps, but I was, above all, Ma's daughter and therefore her abject subject. I could not do anything to stop her.

My vow as a youngster "to be a good little girl," was evolving. My fear of being caught in Ma's web of criminality made me realize that I couldn't trust anyone but myself, which resulted in a hardened streak of independence.

Nineteen

I am playing with Doris, a younger child, who lives upstairs in our apartment building. While we cut out and dress paper dolls, I am aware of a conversation between her parents who assume I do not understand Yiddish. In their exchange, they worry that, because of my mother's unsavory notoriety, I might be a bad influence for Doris. To their great credit, this couple decides to allow our relationship to continue. I don't have many friends, and this decision is important to me.

Fifty years later, after being reacquainted with Doris and exchanging stories about our childhood, she revealed that her mother would tell her that if any man came into my house while we were playing there, she was to leave and bring me upstairs with her for ice cream. In a way, her mother was my savior, at least for that moment.

Ma always spent Saturdays with her current boyfriend, and unless I was enlisted as babysitter for my cousin Dennis, I was usually left at home in lonely isolation. So I developed a very short list of neighborhood kids to invite to the movies. One mother always required me to give a summary of the movie's contents before she would allow her daughter to see it with me. This kind of careful monitoring now seems exceedingly comical, since my own parents had never shown any interest in controlling my exposure to adult situations either in the movies or in the raw reality of my daily existence. It is amusing to imagine the reaction of that careful mother if she learned what I had already seen and heard in my young life.

On a movie day, my friend and I first walked to lunch at Simco's, the popular Mattapan stand, and ate their juicy hot dogs, curbside. Then we went to the ornate Oriental theatre, referred to as the "Ori," with its twinkling stars, moving clouds and Buddhas with lit red and green eyes. It featured two movies with accompanying cartoons, newsreel, and short subjects, all for 12 cents. At some matinees we eagerly collected the dishes that were given away, hoping eventually to complete a set.

When I got home at 5:30, another Saturday had successfully passed with absolutely no guidance, censorship, or interference from my parents. But I had served as a trusted arbiter of morals for a friend whose mother was concerned with the suitability of her daughter's viewing choices. Whatever my confusion about such conflicting views of parental roles, the main thing that has stayed with me was the relief from the unrelenting loneliness of being left at home alone on a Saturday. It was a situation to be avoided at all costs and keeping away that emptiness was often my principal motivation for making and keeping friends.

It was a miracle when, at age eight, I made my first best friend, Karen. A classmate, she was not only smart and popular, she was pretty. I was amazed that her house had so many rooms. I thought it was magnificent. Best of all, the living room was nowhere near her parents' bedroom! Her father was a furrier and her mother was a homemaker who taught me how to make delicious brownies. Karen had toys, dolls, doll carriages, and music lessons. Her household provided me the kind of warm feeling I seldom found in my own. I went to her house every day after school and spending many weekends with her family. To my mind, they were perfect and I often pretended that her family was actually mine.

Other little girls might have noticed Karen's clothes or whether her hair was curly or straight. I noticed how clean her father was, how he supported his family, and that he never lay around the house. Karen's mother was not in business of any kind and was always home when the girls were there. She baked, served us snacks, and kept the house looking like a movie set. The main concern in Karen's household focused on the immoral behavior and growing influence of a young southern rock and roll singer named Elvis Presley, whose swiveling hips, bedroom eyes, hypnotic rhythms, and hoards of screaming teenage fans, seemed to be turning contemporary society on its ear.

I made it a practice to never invite Karen or any other girls to my house. It was simply too risky. I had no idea why I ultimately took such an enormous step, but I finally mustered the courage to invite her for a one-time-only sleepover. That night, Ma prepared dinner for us. The places were set with paper napkins—some of which had already been used—and she served baked chicken pies that remained still frozen in the center. An inappropriate dessert of canned stewed figs further added to my misery. Ma saw Karen as someone she did not need to impress. I had fooled myself into thinking that Ma might magically conform to my wish for normalcy.

Eventually when Karen's family began to plan activities that did not include me, and she became less and less available, it dawned on me that her parents were breaking up our friendship. I realized with a sinking heart that my family's infamy must have reached their ears, but ironically, Ma and I unwittingly delivered the *coup de grace* to our camaraderie.

Most households in our neighborhood spend summers in Nantasket, a South Shore beach town. Karen's family is no exception. The town is not in our universe, but I nag until I am able to convince Ma that I cannot survive the summer unless I, too, can go to Nantasket. Obligingly, Ma rents a room for me in a private home and says she will give me money for restaurant meals and I will be able to hang out with Karen and the other kids. But on the day I am to be dropped off at my rented room, Karen's mother calls Ma at home and asks her to stop first at their beach house and have me wait in the car. When Ma returns, she seems a bit stunned, but is, nevertheless, thoroughly composed. She tells me that Karen's mother berated her about the plan and threatened to call the authorities. I know with certainty that the family has finally had its fill of my family's lifestyle. It is the end of a joy-filled friendship that for four years has meant so much to me in my young life.

I had a tough exterior, but underneath that shell was a kid who dreaded the thought of eating her meals alone in a restaurant and setting up housekeeping with strangers. Chances are, I would most likely have been homesick and gone home early in the summer. It is possible that Ma believed she acted only out of love. She had plenty of confidence in my ability to operate autonomously, although I was only twelve. But no matter what Ma's intentions were, Karen's parents could not justify such a massive failure of parental responsibility. To them, the plan for my summer was a recipe for child neglect, pure and simple.

I was left trying to play the part of a light-hearted, unburdened kid. After this sorry episode, my conclusion was that the family's stain, which marked me as different, loomed much bigger and more obtrusive than I had previously comprehended.

Then there was my brief fling as a Girl Scout. If I had been free to choose, I would undoubtedly have stayed in this giggling sisterhood of cookie sales, green uniforms, and merit badges until boys and dances and makeup lured us all away from its devoted ranks. I was not given such an opportunity or any chance for rebuttal when my Girl Scout leader called Ma and used her notorious reputation as the sole reason why I must immediately withdraw from membership. In her comments to Ma, she alluded to "complaints" from other mothers who did not want their children influenced by the daughter of a hooker. The ax fell hard. I was totally crushed.

Today, I still mull over this outrageous act by an adult and wonder who and how many decided that I was to be singled out as potentially a bad influence on the other girls. Did anyone object to this horrifying decision to tar me or was I exiled out of unanimous sanctimony? I wonder, did anyone think to remind this leader that I was an innocent child? Even then, I was able to reason that they were hysterical vigilantes, thinking I would harm their little darlings, but that didn't thwart the shame and embarrassment I felt. I was a lovely little darling myself and didn't anyone see or care? How could they do this to me? After all, this was the Girl Scouts, society's elite sorority for young girls to flourish and learn. Ma was upset but passed the rejection off as, "Who needs them anyway?"

Whose parents would be the next ones to learn my history and object to me being friends with their children or my membership in a group? It seemed that I would never again allow myself to embrace a friendship as fully as I had with Karen. It was that loss of faith and innocence that triggered a lifelong pattern of mistrust.

As a young married woman, I still heard that hum of uncertainty reminding me of my family's shame. If a new acquaintance asked my maiden name or where I grew up, I often pretended not to hear the question. The anonymity of being born a Cohen or a Levine was not available to me. I was a Winik, and my address was as infamous as my name. If I was cornered and had to answer the question, I often thought I detected a glint of recognition in the questioner's facial expression or body language. That glint instantly became a flashing neon light for me, spelling out: *The notorious WINIKS of Mattapan!* To this day, I continue to be amazed at the comprehensiveness and longevity of my family's reputation.

At the age of fourteen, I suddenly found myself pursued by Barry, a handsome, eighteen-year-old high school senior. He dazzled me on our first date when we doubled with his cousin, Dickie, and a girl named Puppy. We went to *The Bridge on the River Kwai,* followed by dinner at a Chinese restaurant. The only things that marred an otherwise perfect evening was Dickie's barely perceptible snicker and the knowing looks the two boys exchanged when they entered our apartment to pick me up.

Soon Barry and I were going steady. I do not know what other girls my age were doing sexually, but in spite of what the gossips might have said. I did not want to become my mother's mirror image, and had already set my own guidelines for dating behavior. The usual teenage make-out sessions in drive-in theatres or at home was where it began and ended with me. Fortunately, although Barry was older, he did not make sexual demands, and our sweet relationship blossomed.

After his graduation, Barry entered Boston University and pledged Alpha Epsilon Pi, a Jewish fraternity. Not many parents would have allowed their tenth grade daughter to attend fraternity parties, but I entered Barry's new world freely, with no parental restrictions. While most high school sophomores might have felt justifiably intimidated by the presence of older girls at such parties, I mainly felt relief. They were strangers, and therefore didn't know me or my family's reputation! I could relax and enjoy myself. Of course, they may not have felt particularly interested in me anyway, since I was still dressing at my age level and did not have the polish or sophistication of a college girl.

Barry's mother had died before I met him, and his father had remarried and moved to New York, leaving his son to live with an aunt in Dorchester. When the aunt told Barry's dad about our relationship, those familiar neon lights flipped on immediately. His dad delivered an ultimatum to his son: "Stop dating that girl." Further, he said he would force Barry to withdraw from BU and live in New York with him if he did not comply. Then he sweetened the pot with the promise of a new car. Neither Barry's aunt nor his father had ever met me, but they were not willing to let him "risk his future" on a girl from a family such as mine.

Barry pretended to bow to his father's pressure and agreed to stop dating me, but we continued secretly. I was touched by his devotion, and felt that he had done something rather noble. But he was understandably becoming more absorbed in college life, and we soon broke up. Though our break-up was amicable, I emerged from it feeling battle-fatigued and brittle.

How odd it seems that the very things that plague us as children can perversely become part of our parental repertoire. When my own children were growing up they occasionally had playmates whose families had questionable reputations, and I found my maternal antennae vibrating with uncertainty. I wondered, "Should I keep my kids away from such tainted children?" What a pathetic irony that was! The memory of the pain of my early rejections was as intense as it had ever been, and yet I found myself hesitating before welcoming these innocent child victims into our lives.

Twenty

My earliest memories of Daddy's family are the times we gathered together with my uncles, aunts, and cousins in Mucky's living room. We huddled around the four foot, brown magic box, named Philco, with its two big dials, rounded top and large speaker at the bottom. We laughed with *Fibber McGee and Molly* and *The Jack Benny Show* and were entranced by the adventures of *The Shadow* and *Gang Busters*.

Everyone looked forward to holiday celebrations at Mucky's where the focus was on her extraordinary meals. I remember her feasts as a source of *gemütlichkeit*—a feeling of belonging and comfort that I did not often experience elsewhere. Her baked matzo balls attained such stature in my mind that, to this day, I am still trying to duplicate them. Their magical aroma always made me want to stay overnight after the feast so that the next day I could once again fill myself with their curative power. The only exception occurred when I stuffed myself with so many that I cried in discomfort, bitterly disappointed that such a wondrous delicacy could actually hurt me.

Daddy's first taste of the year's batch of homemade horseradish was a favorite annual ritual at Mucky's table. Nobel didn't invent dynamite—Mucky did! Nobel took the time to write down his formula, but Mucky never did, and each batch was different and surprising. During the tasting, Daddy always pretended that his head was going to explode. And each time we saw this pantomime, we shrieked with laughter as if we had never before seen him perform this slapstick routine.

"Why is this night different from all other nights?"

Our 1954 Passover celebration at Mucky's starts out like every other—a splendid feast with the youngest kids asking the traditional four questions and all of us participating in the usual race to find the hidden matzo. I am wearing my new spring clothes to the Seder and basking in the delectable cooking smells and good humor of all the Winik family members.

Between courses, the women start to clear the table, and, apparently, Ma does not move to help quickly enough to suit Uncle Becky. Becoming wild-eyed and red-faced, he suddenly unleashes a loud, uncontrolled tirade directed at her: "You goddamn lazy bitch! You fucking whore! You don't fool anyone!"

The words reverberate in a deafening roar in that room, and we fall silent, stunned, and paralyzed in our seats. Ma says nothing, nor does Daddy. Becky has given words to thoughts that we ourselves can never utter. As Becky begins to calm down, Frances pulls him and their kids into the living room, and soon they all act as if nothing has happened.

Pasey and his family hover around Rowena and me, pretending they have not noticed anything amiss. But, poor Mucky is in a state of suspended animation, not knowing which son or which family to attend to.

Slowly, one-by-one, we leave my grandmother's cherished family holiday celebration with the certain knowledge that it will be our last.

Twenty-One

In a musty pile of nightclub pictures I stare for a very long time at Rowena's gentle, fifteen-year-old face. The photo captures the three of us sitting at a table in Boston's Latin Quarter. I am happy, clearly thrilled to be with my sister and Ma, who is dolled up in her slinky metallic-looking grey silk dress. Rowena—wearing a crisp white blazer—is sweetly smiling and without the slightest inkling that in less than a year she will be homeless on the streets of Boston.

After Rowena returned from the psychiatric hospital, her outward physical appearance became extreme. She looked, carried herself, and routinely dressed like a man—playing to a full-blown "bull-dyke" stereotype. In a rare move for the repressed 50s, my sister had come out of the closet for the entire world to see. Her new appearance was shocking to me. I studied her enthusiastic embrace of that mannish look and demeanor, with its "in-your-face" ducktail haircut, man-cut jeans and big shirts. I was overtaken by a sense of embarrassment. This reaction seemed to obliterate my accustomed feeling of pride in my big sister and quashed the joy I wanted to feel at the prospect of once more having her home.

While I struggled to accept these changes, Ma resisted them totally and immediately began energetic attempts to shove Rowena right back into the closet, beginning with Rowena's complete physical makeover. Having no psychic reserves with which to resist our mother's power and resolve, my sister became her Pygmalion. Ma had Rowena's hair bleached platinum blonde, put her on a strict diet, and bought her a new wardrobe of blatantly feminine, sexy clothes. Daddy played along and introduced her to a young man he knew, a doorman at the taxi stand of one of the Boston hotels. He was single, tall, nice looking and affable. He and Rowena actually dated for a while. No problem; living a lie was Rowena's familiar territory and Ma, with all the lies she routinely juggled, was an outstanding mentor.

But my sister could not long embrace our parents' program, and within several months, she began to drift back to the lesbian community for her social life. Ma was disappointed, but she figured out a way to turn Rowena's "relapse" into a golden opportunity. Since she always needed excuses to enable her nighttime adventures, she began driving Rowena to the gay bars and telling Daddy that by doing so, she was trying to control Rowena's comings and goings. Of course, after dropping off her daughter, Ma would continue onward to meet EIJ. However, to solidify Ma's alibi, the two always came home together. Still playing the part he had been conditioned to play, Daddy lay shirtless on his couch and ignored this new version of the familiar charade.

Ma and Daddy couldn't find any new solutions to the problem of Rowena's way of life, and gradually their attitudes began to harden. For them, it was either embrace the blonde hair and the leopard-skin jumpsuits, and have a boyfriend, or leave their household. When Rowena made her choice with no further equivocation, Daddy threw her out of the house in one of his bizarre shows of macho authority. It was the irony of ironies—Rowena was cast out of the family for being honest about her lifestyle.

This time there would be no private detective to look for her, and Rowena innocently rejoiced that she was finally free to find her own future. But at the age of seventeen, she did not fully comprehend the concept of a pyrrhic victory. She withdrew her $264 nest egg from the bank and fled to the community where she thought she would be safe. But, the welcoming committee robbed her of all her savings. Now she had no money, nowhere to go, and no one to help her.

Thus began a period of homelessness in which Rowena wandered the streets of Boston, going from cafeteria to cafeteria, looking for discarded food to eat. When diners started to notice that she was collecting dirty plates and picking out toast crusts and leftover eggs to eat, she simply moved on to the next place until the staring began anew. If she had a dime, she would buy a can of soup and eat it right out of the can. Time hangs heavy on a lost child, and Rowena spent aimless hours going along with other rootless people, sleeping on the sidewalks, and sometimes sleeping at strangers' group pads.

She was raped twice during this period—once by a boy she thought was a friend, and another time by an angry, brutal, friend-of-a-friend who beat her up during the four-hour rape and threatened to come back for more. He left her whimpering, writhing in pain, and terrified that he would honor his cruel threat. After the rape, Rowena was helped by a man named George, a working man known on the street as a good person and champion of gay women. He let her sleep on his bed and eat his food until she was psychologically strong enough to go back out on her own. Leaving for his bakery job the morning after the rape,

George gestured to a box of oatmeal, indicating that she was welcome to have some for breakfast. But in her crisis of pain, misery, and confusion, Rowena had no idea how to cook it, so she huddled miserably in the empty room and nibbled distractedly on the dry, coarsely ground oats.

It was growing colder in Boston and Rowena had no winter coat to keep away winter's onslaught. Someone— another faceless acquaintance—kindly loaned her his camel-colored topcoat. She was wearing this coat when she passed a familiar cafeteria and saw Bubbe and Moishe sitting at a table, eating. She stared at them longingly; desperate to run over and embrace them, but she held back and didn't go because she was ashamed of having them see her.

Rowena had a friend whose job included doing markdowns at Filene's Bargain Basement. If she saw a nice sweater or pants that might fit my sister, she would set them aside until the price went down as low as it could go. And then she would purchase them for pennies and take them to Rowena, suggesting that it would be a good idea for her to modify her appearance to a preppier, sportier coordinated style of slacks or skirts and sweaters for the sake of getting a decent job. Acquiring clothes was only one of the issues Rowena faced. The need for sanitary napkins and other personal items presented a continuing problem, and she was always on the alert for ways to steal them from bathrooms. However, she had lost so much weight that her periods came only occasionally, and sometimes, not at all.

Dale, my little sister, you asked about my homelessness and I will tell you the best way I can. At first, I thought our parents were making a mountain out of a mole hill. It wasn't a big deal. They didn't understand me, didn't understand the racial issue, and didn't have any idea about what it meant to be gay. I thought they were dumb, ignorant, and didn't get any of it. I didn't think they were much different from any other parents who didn't understand their kid. But then I realized that what had happened to me was a huge issue—after all, the whole Commonwealth of Massachusetts was coming down on me.

Ma was quick to turn Rowena's absence into an advantage when she began spinning a set of lies designed to impress the neighbors. She told everyone that Rowena had become an airline stewardess, and was now happily married to a pilot and traveling the globe. When, on one extremely rare occasion, Rowena briefly visited us at Revere Beach, I stood by and watched the neighborhood *yentas* (gossips) gathering around to greet her. They immediately figured out that she could not possibly be living the life Ma had described, and, like scavengers, they greedily ripped at the carcass of lies and licked their lips in anticipation of spreading the word of Rowena's failure to thrive.

My sister began a succession of low level jobs, starting with one at an all-girl carwash where she was paid 25 cents an hour and was assigned the repetitive task of wiping the right rear fenders of cars passing by in monotonous succession. In those days, an "outed" lesbian didn't just walk into an office and say she wanted to work the telephones or do typing and filing. Rowena knew that most of the people who dressed like her were plucking chicken feathers in a factory in the South End. She was beginning to learn that to make it to the inside of an office, she had to soften her look and acquire the clothing and mannerisms common among all the other people in that work environment—regardless of their sexual identity. With this adaptation, she wasn't really going back in the closet; she was, in effect, practicing her own version of the military's compromise policy of *don't ask, don't tell*—a concept which wasn't to appear until 1993.

After this desultory passage in her young life, Rowena somehow found the strength to return home for a year or so in order to get a high school degree from Newman Preparatory School in Boston, paid for by Ma. She then spent a semester at Boston University with Ma pressuring her to get her degree as quickly and as inexpensively as possible. The guilt and the pressure must have weighed heavily on my sister, because she left college after only one semester and then left home for good. Our contact was severely limited for the next twenty years. The few times I did see Rowena, she was often volatile and unapproachable in our family's presence, and I had no idea what to offer or say to her. As far as I could tell, the only thing that still held us together was that deep and tender connection we both remembered from our early lives.

Ma, you were never ashamed of any of your own outrageous behavior, but you tried every trick in your book to hide Rowena's lifestyle. Did you forget all those years when Rowena helped you cling to the fantasy that gave you legitimacy by lying for you and protecting you? You had convinced yourself that you were Mattapan's Miss Gypsy Rose Lee who stripped for the enjoyment of men and was beloved for it. I am sure your men enjoyed your attention. No matter, Ma, the important thing for you was that they all paid a price for admission. Why was it that you never felt disgraced by your own behavior, but allowed yourself to feel disgraced by Rowena's? By what twisted standard did you exonerate yourself and then turn around to convict your own daughter?

Rowena often imagines herself confronting you and asking how you can live with the truth. But she doesn't have to; she knows what your answer is. She knows you would say, "Mein kindt (my child), don't worry about me, I am tougher than that; the men are nothing, those assholes. Who cares?" In her imaginings, Rowena always gazes deep into your beautiful green eyes and says, "I do, Mama. I care."

Ma   **Daddy**

Daddy, Rowena, Dale, Ma

Dale, Rowena   **Ma, Dale**

Ma   **Dale, Rowena, Ma**
at Latin Quarter

Part Two

Ring around the rosy
A pocketful of posies;
"Ashes, Ashes"
We all Fall Down!

Twenty-Two

From the shadows, Ma makes me laugh and shudder alternatively—stealing my concentration whenever she can. I am charmed, drawn into that magnetic aura by her enthusiasm and zany love of life, and feel warmth and belonging in her presence. But just as suddenly, I feel the pain of all her contradictions: the lies, schemes, and petty crimes, the apparent indifference and the poor judgment that affects us so profoundly. I have finally learned to resist the temptation to view the past with despair, but still, when memories crowd in on me too fast, I occasionally lose ground.

In keeping with my rapidly evolving grownup aura and recently acquired smoking habit, my girlfriends eschewed the customary teddy bear gifts for my sweet-sixteen birthday. Instead they gave me a shiny gold metal cigarette case engraved with my new nickname, *Foxy.*

Just who was *Foxy*? I was not cool like I imagined my façade projected, but rather a frightened, insecure teenager. Acting like a know-it-all was my defense mechanism.

Ma was not in any way qualified to lead me through the turbulence and bewilderment of my teenage years, so she treated me as a twenty-five-year-old confidante instead. In the process, I began to acquire the aura I knew best—hers. I already bore a strong physical resemblance to her but now that I was applying daily makeup by the pound, the likeness seemed all the more striking.

Strange men sometimes approached me, "Hey, you must be May's daughter! Wanna get together?" My reply to such invitations was always filled with righteous indignation. Inside, I was completely mortified, and as soon as the inquiring stranger withdrew, I ran away like a spooked deer. The overriding imperative was that I did not want to turn out like Ma.

However, in attitude and appearance, I was becoming May's clone. We were spending a lot of time together, often singing Ma's favorite Yiddish songs, or frenetically dancing around the apartment to the mambo and the cha-cha.

She decreed me her grooming consultant and hair-dresser, allowing me to decide how her hair looked best and expecting me to do the styling. I relished my self-appointed role of *maven* (expert). We shared fashion know-how and wore each other's clothes—no matter that hers were too grown-up for me and mine were too youthful for her. On special dates, I now had carte blanche to wear any of Ma's sexy black cocktail dresses.

Ma loved the Concord Hotel in upstate New York, the largest, glitziest and one of the most famous in the Borscht Belt. In those days, major celebrities sang, danced, and joked their way to stardom on the stages of hotel nightclubs. Show business celebrities like Don Rickles, Tony Bennett, Milton Berle, Tony Martin and Sid Caesar worked their magic. Guests stuffed themselves with the tasty kosher food. "We'll have the chopped liver and please bring stuffed cabbage and knishes for the whole table to sample. I'll have lamb chops, potato pancakes and a little *flanken* (stewed or boiled beef) on the side," "By the way, how is the salmon?" The waiter rolls his eyes. "I'll bring you some of that too." Thus was the Jewish gastronomic experience.

Ma made many pilgrimages there with her loyal posse— including me, of course. Though I was only sixteen, I desperately wanted to work at the Concord. I was sure that my hip attitude would fit in with the flashy New Yorkers. Ma gave me her blessing to do so and I was eventually hired as a dining room hostess in the summer before my senior year in high school. I showed up for work with newly-tinted red hair, a wardrobe of provocative clothing, and a big attitude. But I quickly learned that as soon as I officially became an employee, the fabled Catskill glitz no longer applied to me. Instead, I endured long shifts six days a week, sixteen hours a day—with very little down time, meager wages, and no tips—and then fell exhausted into bed in a dingy dormitory. The wait staff consisted of college kids. But such was my insecurity that I made no friends among them. This time, I wasn't worried that they would find out about my mother's reputation, I was worried they might perceive my own flaws.

I was far happier as a guest than as an employee, and was tired of being homesick and physically exhausted. Having thus evaluated my circumstances, I packed up after six weeks and went home to Ma. I felt I failed the challenge of being grown-up and able to separate myself from home.

Not long after I returned from working at the Concord, I received a call from a guy named Sonny who was a friend of a friend. When he turned up for our blind date, I was pleasantly surprised to see that he was a handsome guy with a warm smile and a nice physique. I was instantly smitten, and it never even occurred to me to wonder why a twenty-four-year-old guy was interested in a sixteen-year-old girl. I simply accepted that my newly-acquired sophisticated attitude was tailor-made for Sonny's highly-charged style. We began to date with a vengeance and soon became a "happening" couple who frequented the Cave, a Latin dance club known for its fast patronage. Soon, we were recognized at the trendy restaurants and at the late night hot spots where we did our drinking.

It would have been absurd to expect Sonny to socialize with high school seniors or attend my prom. So I unwisely became estranged from the few high school friends I had left, telling myself that I was above all that stuff anyway. And so, a previously lonely, insecure hooker's daughter struggling with her identity was now the puffed-up girlfriend of a tough guy wannabe.

Twenty-Three

It is a recurring dream... Ma, Daddy, Ma's boyfriend, and I are huddled together like a pack of wolves. There is lots of chatter and commotion. Ma's boyfriend is sitting at the kitchen table with his broken arm in a sling. I feel bad for him but ashamed he is part of our household. I ask him, "Isn't it terrible that we live like this?" He immediately shushes me up, saying that I am being disrespectful. He is as needy as I am.

What could you possibly be thinking, Daddy? Don't you know husbands and boyfriends don't live together?

The mayhem frightens me. If I flee, where will I go and what will I do? I charge out of the apartment to start my own life but find the car has been stolen. I come back to report the theft. I am trapped.

I began to develop some small pockets of self-esteem, which Ma did not hesitate to pickpocket from even that nascent supply. I was no longer the little girl being forced to pass her mother's johns in the hallway. Nevertheless, I was just as likely to meet Ma on the dance floor with one of her current boyfriends. I soon realized that these encounters were not by chance; Ma had apparently entered into a strange, twisted competition with me. She had gone through her share of guys over the years and some of them—like EIJ and Sam—actually became part of our lives, for better or for worse. But now a new boyfriend, Billy, had entered, and he brought with him more excitement and gangster burlesque than all her previous boyfriends combined. He was single, good-looking in a weasel kind of way, and fully fifteen years younger than Ma. When they met, he was grinding out a living with his taxi, barely staying ahead of his mounting gambling debts. The two of them connected instantly, not just sexually, but also through their mutual attraction to flimflam and larceny. They were a perfect match.

In order to compensate for a pair of badly deformed legs and a Ratso Rizzo-like gait, Billy had a rough guy persona with a large dose of braggadocio and an unending string of stories of alleged underworld connections. I don't think any of us believed his mafia stories; instead, we considered him a petty wheeler-dealer. Looking back, I realize that Billy and Sonny shared very similar reasons for their bravado and that Ma and I were their willing enablers.

Ma brought Billy home to meet us. But when she introduced him to Daddy, she said unblinkingly that she wanted to set him up with Rowena in hopes that she would "go straight." Of course, Rowena was not living with us, and hadn't for a number of years, but that little detail didn't deter Ma a bit. She was able to hoodwink Daddy into accepting the ruse—or perhaps Daddy hadn't the energy or desire to raise an objection—and Billy immediately began hanging around just enough to get Daddy accustomed to having him in our home.

Ma and Billy soon formed a business partnership and eventually acquired 30 taxis in a highly-leveraged operation. Ma supplied the necessary capital and Billy ran the day-to-day functions, hiring drivers, collecting the money and maintaining the cabs. Daddy continued to operate independently in the taxi Ma had bought for him and never became a part of the venture.

Inevitably, Ma became uncomfortable with using her own money as capital and came up with a devilish idea. She sweet-talked Billy into moving into our apartment with us, telling him that would enable them to "spend more time together." But she had a more sinister motive. She made sure that Billy came home right after work—before he counted the day's take—and she routinely stole handfuls of cash from the moneybags he brought with him. Since he hadn't yet tallied the amount, Billy never knew the difference. The plan was a winner for Ma and ensured an unusually healthy return on her original investment. She continued doing this—without being discovered—for the several years Billy stayed with us. She managed to keep Daddy's acquiescence with the living arrangement, by telling him about the scam she was waging against "Rowena's boyfriend."

It would be hard to imagine a more unique living arrangement than the one that unfolded. During the night, Billy slept on our living room sofa while it was still warm from Daddy's body. Then, in a variation on the familiar theme from my childhood, Ma joined Billy on the sofa for sex after Daddy left for work. Once again, I was stuck in my bedroom waiting for Ma to finish her ministrations. I tried making my presence known by coughing or yawning and resumed the same kind of weak admonishments I had made as a child. Eventually, I became bolder and told Ma that it was thoughtless of them to behave this way with me in the apartment. But Ma continued to do just as she wished. She couldn't care less about offending my youthful sensibilities. No surprise there.

Why did I continue to live at home, putting up with all this? Why didn't I leave home as Rowena had so many years before? Simply stated, I was afraid of what would happen to me. As always, I fell back into the role of the compliant, "good and loyal" daughter. Ma continued to generously share with me all the unseemly and unwelcome details of her complicated sex/love life.

I was not the only one who couldn't rid herself of Ma's accustomed modus operandi. Even when Rowena was in her forties, she had trouble overcoming the conditioning that Ma had put in place when we were young and impressionable. She recalled a time when she went to Ma's place to pick her up for an outing and noticed that a john was in the hallway outside Ma's bedroom. Like the helpless child she once was, she dutifully sat down, folded her hands, and waited for Ma to finish. Rowena knew she was somehow incapable of leaving, and angrily thought to herself, "You've got to be out of your fucking mind to be staying here!" Of course, when Ma came out of her bedroom and the john had left, she was completely at ease, and nothing was said about the situation. Rowena's early training as Ma's loyal serf was still firmly in place.

Twenty-Four

Although I was enrolled in the college prep course in high school, I had never discussed with Ma and Daddy the notion of attending college. Why would I have even brought it up? They placed little value whatsoever on higher education and did not know or care enough to offer any encouragement or guidance for my academic future. If I needed any proof of this, all I had to do was remember Rowena's catastrophic departure from high school. Many of my friends were using their parents' occupations as a natural stepping stone to making their own career choices. If my father was a lawyer, perhaps I'd study law. If my mother was a school teacher, I might go into education. Given my environment it would have meant aspiring to be either a cab driver or hooker. So I was rudderless and on my own, and as a consequence, facing graduation without a plan or direction of any kind.

After graduation, in 1961, I enrolled in Burdett College, a two-year secretarial school and after my first day, a wave of guilt spread over me. All night long I thrashed and turned in bed and could not sleep. Questions were popping into my mind. How was Ma going to afford this? Surely Daddy was no help. Will it be worth it? I woke up in the morning, exhausted from the night's mental exercise, marched off to Burdett and quit.

Plan B: I set my sights on Boston Business School in Roxbury, which targeted disadvantaged high school graduates and offered them a free education. In those days, the label "disadvantaged" did not enhance the status of a school the way it might in the more enlightened present. "I'm not disadvantaged. Don't I go to Florida on vacations? Aren't I modish? Look at my red hair!" I viewed the place as not worthy of my time and efforts, but, I was saving Ma money. I stayed for six months and then quit, convinced that I could make my own way with the skills I managed to pick up in that short time.

I had very little to sell an employer other than my good looks and basic street smarts. As I was extremely unsure and ill-equipped for presenting myself in a professional setting, I participated in a string of awkward interviews which did not produce results. But eventually, I was hired as a receptionist for a manufacturing company. What I lacked in experience I soon made up for with a strong work ethic and a willingness to take on responsibility. After a year, I was promoted to executive secretary to the president. This promotion went to my head, and I began to think of myself as having nothing in common with the rest of the staff. I viewed them the way Ma viewed most "normal" outsiders —as chumps.

In search of broader horizons, I decided to leave the company. However, I lacked a clear plan and spent a lot of time lolling around the apartment mired in a case of mild depression. I finally told Ma that I was feeling uncomfortably sad, and she called our Ob/Gyn doctor who suggested that amphetamines would perk me up and get me out of the doldrums. They were the drug of choice in those days, and were easy to acquire. Ma herself was an expert in their use as she had experienced a bout of depression several years before—possibly because of her life choices—and found that they made her feel happy and vital again. Thus I began a habit that continued for the next four years until I recognized that these drugs could lead to big problems and stopped taking them.

Eventually, word got around to my ex-boss that I had not yet found a job, and he called to offer me my job back, sweetening the deal with a $10-a-week increase. With no better deal before me, I returned to my former office, and in the process, foolishly bragged to everyone about my unprecedented raise. My co-workers weren't naturally inclined to be happy for me and promptly staged a revolt to protest what they considered my unfair advantage. My boss fired me immediately because I had not been smart enough to keep my big mouth shut.

My cheek enabled me to be hired as a legal secretary, in a one-person office, even though I lacked the proper background. Without other staff people around, I felt no pressure to dazzle the multitudes, and poured all my energy into enjoying both the work and my employer. For two years we worked closely together, as he taught and I learned. My undisputed success in this office was a morale booster, and I gradually began to feel capable and appreciated. My boss confidently loaned me out to other law offices in the building if our work was caught up and they needed additional help. I didn't realize it at the time, but my success in a "one-girl" office was part of an emerging pattern. Not wanting to be rejected, I generally remained aloof from other people. It seemed to me that such isolation worked well as a protective shield.

Twenty-Five

Billy never caught onto Ma's skimming activities. He was busy with his own scams. I had long been aware that he had an unending supply of vending machine and pay phone slugs, but I had not anticipated his more serious criminal involvement in a stolen car ring. Eventually, I found out that he was filling orders with stolen cars. Even his personal car—a showy navy blue Cadillac convertible with a powder blue top—was stolen. As the operation grew, a scenario evolved that was worthy of the Broadway classic, "Guys and Dolls," complete with Billy's own ridiculous version of the play's illegal floating crap game which exploited the godly Save-a-Soul mission.

The stolen cars had to be stored until the serial numbers could be expunged, and the cars delivered to customers. But keeping the hot merchandise at the cab garage could jeopardize his legitimate business, so he scouted our neighborhood looking for an appropriate place to rent. When he brazenly chose the unused garage of our next-door neighbor—an orthodox rabbi of a large congregation in Dorchester—the sheer absurdity of the situation took my breath away. While the rabbi was living a life of rectitude and service to others, totally unaware of what was going on, Billy was busy stashing his ill-gotten gains right under his nose! I often pictured the rabbi hunched over, diligently planning his next religious sermon, while his garage doors were opening wide and disgorging an unending parade of hot cars into the night. One thing about Billy, he had audacity to spare. Fortunately, the stolen car ring fizzled before any arrests were made, and the rabbi was never the wiser.

As ridiculous as the stolen car caper was, it seems equally absurd that during this period of my life, Sonny and I occasionally double-dated with Ma and Billy while my cuckolded father stayed at home, lying on the couch. I do not know what was going on in my mind when I acquiesced to this shocking arrangement. It must have been my peculiar adaptation to Ma's need to feel "cool and sexy," and my constant need to win her approval. How else can I explain my participation in such a sleazy foursome? Oddly enough, there were other times when Ma and Billy arrived unannounced at The Cave to dance and mingle with my friends, and in the process, managed to infuriate me. She had long ago blurred all the lines between mother and daughter, but this intrusion into a space Sonny and I thought was "our world" rankled, and made me wonder if I would ever escape my mother's grasp. It seemed that, after one boundary had been breached, we lost the entire concept of limits and taboos. As irrational as it all was, it was left to me to explain Billy to my friends. I would pass him off as a business acquaintance but Ma's reputation was too wide spread to fool anyone.

One day, Billy fondly bought Ma a Chihuahua named Poco which soon became the focus of an insane amount of attention from all three adults in the Ma-Daddy-Billy love triangle. Daddy showed more interest in that dog than he did to his children. Ma paraded around with the little dog under her arm, drawing attention to herself wherever she went. Poco wore sunglasses, a Chiquita banana hat with dangling fruit, or a golf hat and a matching leather shirt collar—just a sampling of his vast canine wardrobe. This all occurred decades before Paris Hilton made her own Chihuahuas famous for the same sort of ridiculous anthropomorphism.

I am embarrassed to admit that I actually found myself bathed in jealousy when Ma went so far as to commission an oil portrait of her little dog. She had never displayed pictures of Rowena or me—and she certainly never commissioned any oil portraits of us. We barely had any photographs of ourselves as children other than those nightclub photos with Ma in the spotlight.

During the Billy period, Ma's scam against the cab business yielded even more money than the tricks. She underwrote a series of expensive trips with us, her loyal entourage. We slept in five star hotels in London, Rome, and Paris. We sunned on both the Italian and French Riviera. We won and lost at the blackjack tables in Monte Carlo. We were chauffeured over the mountain roads from Mexico City to Acapulco. And we toured Israel just three years before the '67 War. The list goes on and on. Ma said she was happy to share her exotic odysseys with me, but she also made certain that I complied in the role of plausible decoy in order to fool Daddy. This made it easier for her to take Billy along. Ma wanted to experience the best of what the world had to offer, and it seemed that if she had $10 in her pocket, $1 of that would go for the necessities of living, and the other $9 would go straight to a sampling of some worldly luxuries.

Ma and Daddy's 24' power boat, like Aladdin's Magic Carpet, transports us to Boston's various local islands, and harbors. (Yes, Ma has a boat—it is a necessary luxury in her pursuit of the good life.) Daddy doesn't know where he is going most of the time. Somehow we get there, except for the few occasions the Coast Guard rescues us when we send an SOS from our unidentifiable location. It never occurs to Daddy to take a navigation course.

We enter the beautiful and mighty Boston Harbor, tie up to a pier so Ma and I can buy provisions. Passing us by are seven very cute young Italian sailors whose ship is docked in the harbor. Their generous whistles are flattering substitutes for their inability to speak English. Ma and I can't speak Italian. That doesn't stop us. We wave to them and belt out "Volare," Domenico's Modugno's hit song, crooned in Italian. In response, the sailors chime in lustily, and for five glorious electric minutes, under that brilliant blue sky, we are all in love. I didn't know any sixteen-year-old who would be singing "Volare" with the Italian navy and having so much fun.

I became a legitimate jet setter who enjoyed fancy hotel lobbies and ceviche as much as a good corned beef sandwich, and Ma made it clear that I owed it all to her. How could I complain about my lost youth when Ma had given me the world? But I thought often of how much I envied other girls my age who were dancing with boys at record hops while I was dancing with much older strangers at a faraway hotel or on a cruise ship. I knew that I had become artificial and affected and that my life was a mess. But, I told myself, I loved Ma. Was it so wrong for me to act like her even against my better judgment? Was there anything left of the person I was meant to be? Where were those uncompromising personal standards that allowed me to survive in the upside-down world of my childhood? Ma had devoured me!

Twenty-Six

Now that I was doing well in my one-woman job in a law office, I began to concentrate more on my relationship with Sonny. As our mutual trust grew, he reluctantly revealed that he was a juvenile diabetic and dependent on a daily shot of insulin since the age of fifteen. He was bitter and resentful about his dependency and feared being viewed as weak. I knew what it felt like to feel defective and was used to keeping secrets. I readily agreed to keep his. Because this obsession clouded his outlook and shaped his life, Sonny spent an inordinate amount of time and energy trying to hide his condition. He had acquired a wise guy image to mask any signs of weakness, and by the time we were dating, he had cultivated it to a high art.

When Sonny had a diabetic reaction, unchecked, he could become incoherent. At first, I was frightened, but once I realized how quickly he regained his equilibrium by eating a candy bar or drinking orange juice, it became a matter of routine intervention and prevention on my part. The more difficult challenge for me was to act fast enough—in accordance with Sonny's wishes—to prevent anyone from suspecting or discovering that he had a disability. I certainly did not fully grasp the seriousness of Sonny's illness or the all-consuming anguish he felt. I certainly did not imagine the health consequences he would face as a relatively young man.

Sonny didn't go to college and worked in his uncle's gas station. After a few years, he enrolled in a technical welding program in preparation for a job selling metals and welding supplies. He became the first in his family to join the Masons, and was extremely proud of that honor. To celebrate his accomplishment, I gave him a diamond Masonic ring as a gift. To him, belonging to a fraternity of successful men was a sign that he had surpassed his family's social status. Now that he had me, with my girl-around-town demeanor, heavy makeup, and showy clothes, he became more confident that he looked like a player and that no one could mess with him.

Sonny still lived with his parents in a second floor flat in a modest two-family house in the Jewish neighborhood of Malden. Despite the aura I projected, I was *hamish* (down-to-earth) and participated comfortably in their Shabbat dinners, Sunday restaurant lunches and visits with relatives.

I tried to blend in with the family's dull, lackluster lifestyle but always stood out in that crowd as a flaming non-conformist. When I attended the funeral of Sonny's grandfather with my bleached blonde hair tinted pink, I was a bit embarrassed by my flamboyance, but never even considered putting on a scarf to more appropriately honor the occasion.

Sonny's father, Eddie, a soft spoken gentle man, worked as an office clerk at Blue Cross/Blue Shield. He had once prospered in the hardware business, but his success there became a casualty of the Depression. Sonny's mother, Lillian, constantly reminded her husband of his failures and her disappointment in him.

Lillian was an attractive, rather buxom woman with a beautifully coifed head of silver hair. She continually bragged about her culinary talents (a subjective judgment) and her housekeeping skills (the "whitest wash in the Western Hemisphere"). She was employed as a teller at the local credit union and considered herself a celebrity in that world. As it was not common in her social milieu for that generation of women to have jobs, she used her bank position as the justification for browbeating her husband for his inability to adequately support the family. But, given her vast list of unappealing traits, it was Lillian's obvious lack of affection for almost anyone except her beloved Sonny—Sumner William—that bothered me the most.

Melvin, Sonny's younger brother by five years, was a dull, quiet kid who, even in his mother's eyes, ran a distant second to his brother as a worthy recipient of affection and respect. Mel often sought refuge from the family by being with his girlfriend, Judy, a girl he had dated since junior high and eventually married.

Ma, with her gift of picking ripe fruit from the driest trees, had fun showing off in front of Sonny's family. She needed the roar of the crowd to satisfy her ego, and on one occasion early in our relationship invited Sonny and his parents to stop by for coffee just before we were to attend a wedding. Ma greeted them wearing a long black jersey dress trimmed with a white mink collar. I was at my best in a stunning low-cut lace gown, and Daddy, having risen to the occasion, was dashing in a new suit. As we engaged in small talk over pastries and coffee, Lillian's failure to comment on our attire simply highlighted her withholding, jealous nature and provided a great deal of satisfaction to Ma. The entire visit was staged to showcase what Ma saw as our superiority to Sonny's drab family. Between the two of them, Lillian and Ma broke all the records for obvious character flaws.

Sonny announced his intention to marry me by giving me a hope chest which family and friends filled with lovely sheets, towels, tablecloths, and household appliances. My reaction to the chest gave me a clear view of the dichotomy in my own character. I loved those symbols which provided me a much needed emotional safety net. But, as my mother's cynical daughter, my inner voice mocked my zeal for seeking such a simple-minded solution to my problems.

I spent most of my young life convinced that acquiring a "chicken soup family" would fill the holes in my psyche. However, I had some serious doubts about this particular family, as I was sure they were having about me. Above all, I observed both Lillian's enthusiasm for nasty brow-beating and Sonny's hot temper. For Sonny, our relationship was more about him than us, and he never even tried to discover the fragile young woman beneath the May-inspired physical props. But my endless mission to save myself from what I saw as my certain destiny began to overshadow any unattractive insights I had about Sonny and his family and I was soon trying to sell myself the Brooklyn Bridge.

I foolishly approached Ma for guidance because I was undergoing a lot of doubt and worry about Sonny's health, his mean streak, and my fear that I didn't care that much about him. She was my mother, but it made absolutely no sense for me to seek her advice. What possible suggestions and direction could she give me? My ambivalence was annoying to her. Even though she did not like Sonny and thought of him as bitter, it was easier for her to sell me out to a bad decision than to come up with a thoughtful response to my concerns. So she just impatiently spat out some ill-considered advice: "Oh, just go marry him!" And thus, with these five words, Ma's statement completely devalued my hesitations and qualms, and catapulted me into the decision to marry a man who filled me with foreboding.

Twenty-Seven

Diabetes was Sonny's nemesis, a major factor in his all-consuming paranoia and insecurity. He had a lot to prove to the world and strutted around displaying a hard-hitting male air. This attitude was a major contributor to his ill temper. Those were reasons enough for me to break off the relationship. In retrospect, I realized I was confused and discontented, and had no idea who or what I was looking for, and no idea whose eyes I was looking through.

That summer, when I was nineteen, I met a young man named Al and decided I was wild about him. Although the relationship never went anywhere, I considered my interest in him an important indicator that Sonny was not my dream of the future. This brief moment of clarity enabled me to dig deep enough to find the strength to break my engagement to Sonny. Although he was disappointed about the breakup, he coolly argued that we should continue dating. Since I was still not entirely ready to abandon the security he offered, we agreed to keep seeing one another, but not exclusively.

There followed a desultory period in which I dated a number of forgettable men and further lost my way. Among them was a powerful politician, who was married and considered me a mere diversion. After that, I was intrigued by a 50-year-old married man who turned out to be a customer of Ma's. When I learned this sordid fact, my skin began to crawl. Although I broke off the relationship immediately, I was frightened and realized that I was totally out of my league with both of them. So, I opted out of Ma's age group and started to look for younger men.

While Ma and I were vacationing in Puerto Rico I met Americo Colon Rosa who took us sightseeing during the day and to dinner and dancing at night. He and I danced ourselves into a frenzy and—in an ironic role reversal—Ma was forced to sit on the sidelines watching us. One evening, she made a big point of telling me that she had "the hots" for Americo. He occasionally threw her a bone and danced with her, but she was distraught when he did not throw me aside for her.

During another trip to Puerto Rico with Ma and Billy, I met Phil, a thirty-three-year-old New Yorker, the man of my distorted dreams. He said he liked my chutzpah and my Boston accent. For the remainder of the trip, we had dinner together every night and spent the rest of the evening at the gaming tables. He frequently gave Ma $100 to try her luck, while half-joking that he was trying to get rid of her. But Ma squirreled the money away in her usual way—in the pocket she sewed in the side of all her long line bras for stashing her license, keys and money—rather than squandering it on gambling. By the end of this Puerto Rican interlude, I was hopelessly in love with Phil, and when I returned to Boston, he called me every day and flew in for dinner each week. Phil had access to an elegant Sutton Place apartment in New York and I regularly stayed there with him, surrounded by the mirrored walls of this swanky custom-designed one-room hideaway. A doorman greeted me as I came and went—just like in the movies—but I didn't fool myself that Phil was a legitimate businessman. I assumed he was in the rackets because he always carried wads of cash and wore expensive custom-made suits, monogrammed ice-blue shirts, and ice-blue underwear that knocked my ice-blue socks off! When Phil called for dinner reservations, his favorite foods were waiting for us by the time we arrived at the restaurant. He showered me with the best of New York City's offerings and I was so excited by the experience I was running out of oxygen.

One evening a friend of Phil's invited us to his Park Avenue apartment for a casual dinner served in the kitchen by a maid. The main course was a Viennese specialty— meatloaf with a hard-boiled egg nestled in the center. Notwithstanding all the accoutrements of that gorgeous apartment and its servants, all I could focus on that evening was that egg! But despite the Viennese delicacy, and the opulence of his surroundings, Phil's friend could not keep himself from being sent to jail soon after our memorable dinner in his kitchen.

By now, I was going very fast without applying the brakes. I knew very little about Phil's life, except that he had two children and was separated from his wife. I knew he cared about me, but noticed that he kept me at arm's length emotionally. And since I did not have any friends in New York, I was often alone and very lonely in his apartment while he was doing other things. I can only assume that my tender age of twenty and my underlying neediness put pressure on him, because Phil ended our relationship after a year's romance, saying that he had my best interests at heart. I was miserable, but felt a degree of gratitude towards him for pulling me out of the hole I knew I was in. Intellectually, I knew I was well out of the Phil relationship, but my confidence was badly shaken by the breakup and I was grateful to learn that Sonny was still interested in me. Now, in my confusion, he had never looked better! This time, emotionally battered and bruised, I happily accepted his engagement ring.

Twenty-Eight

Ma threw herself a fabulous bridal shower in honor of my upcoming wedding and, as the bride-to-be; I was merely a prop in her lavish production. I wished she and I could have planned a conventional bridal shower—with bouquets made of bows from opened gifts and friends writing down funny sayings. But simple was not in her vocabulary. Instead, she rented a posh little jazz club and wowed everyone with live music from her favorite band. The dazzled guests paid homage to her choice of a locally celebrated caterer as they ate greedily and then covertly wrapped up the leftovers and mouth-watering pastries to take home. A couple of weeks later, I learned that Ma's generosity with this over-the-top party was really just another of her schemes. She had figured out a way to swindle Billy into paying for most of it! He and the caterer were close friends, so Ma successfully gambled that if she reneged on paying the bill, Billy would quickly cover the debt to avoid cheating a valued friend.

To liven things up, Ma danced around with my sister— yes, Rowena showed up for the event, although she wasn't at all fond of Sonny—with both grandmothers, and Auntie. I noticed with some concern that the rest of the party goers weren't joining in the revelry. Ma had planned a sexy event for unsexy people. Her inappropriateness just reduced my unpretentious new "chicken soup" family members and friends to mere onlookers. Nothing new here; for my whole life I had been watching people gawking at the Winik freaks. But in those days, I had bought into Ma's philosophy of us against them. Other people were the *shlemiels* (fools); we were the *machers* (big shots). But now, those people were to become my family. Perhaps for the first time, I was absorbing the full effect of Ma's flamboyant and thoughtless behavior. I had plenty of doubts on a number of fronts about my upcoming marriage, but now I was even more afraid of the destiny that awaited me if I did not marry Sonny as soon as possible.

Not satisfied with the first bash, Ma was also hell bent on hosting an engagement celebration. It was held in Swampscott, at the New Ocean House, one of the great old resort hotels of the early 20th century. What was the real reason for her unnecessary emotional and financial investment? Certainly it wasn't all for those *shleppers* (low class/simple people) in Sonny's family, and obviously it wouldn't impress Sonny's aunt with the Communist husband. But when Ma showed me the new black beaded cocktail coat she planned to wear, I understood immediately. It was all about her. I was completely outmatched.

Not wanting to make Ma spend a lot on my wedding, I planned an uncomplicated ceremony in the study of Ma's favorite rabbi, followed by a small family dinner. The simplicity of the service appealed to Ma but she rejected my idea of a small family dinner. No, she said, we would have a full wedding reception at the Colonial Hotel in Wakefield with Ma acting as the mistress of the estate.

My wedding day was an opportunity for me to immerse myself in traditional values and show the world the person I really was, but I had no idea how to do that, and I certainly did not know who I really was. I bypassed the more modest bridal tradition of the times—sleeves and a very modest show of skin—and selected a dramatic long, white spaghetti strap dress and wrapped my hair with pearls, emulating an Egyptian headpiece with one large tear-shaped bead hanging over my forehead. It was an exotic look for which I was lavished with compliments. Not surprisingly, Ma outdid herself for the occasion and wore a strapless chocolate brown chiffon gown with an orange, yellow, and red cascade. Rowena, as my maid of honor, was beautiful in a pink and rose embroidered gown that she chose herself. Lillian made a point of remarking to no one in particular that my white dress was inappropriate since Sonny and I had "traveled" together long before the wedding.

According to a Jewish custom, Sonny and I were put in a room alone together briefly after the ceremony to "get to know one another" in a symbolic way with a glass of champagne. Then, when we emerged, the wedding party poured out of the rabbi's humble house onto the street where Billy awaited—in the front seat of his swanky stolen Cadillac with its top down—to drive us to the hotel. The contrast between the rabbi's-blessed purity of my traditional marriage ceremony and the sight of Billy waiting for us in his stolen car outside the rabbi's house was just another instance of my family's penchant for burlesque.

We kicked up our heels at the wedding reception where Ma's favorite band was playing again. Uncle Pasey was our event photographer, and as an unexpected bonus, he and Aunt Edna surprised us with an impromptu dance routine.

Amid all this celebration, Lillian and her sisters lay in wait for Rowena like predators hiding in the tall grass. They called her over to their table, pretended innocence, and asked her where her husband, the pilot, was. They wanted to see Rowena squirm. Rowena saw their inquisition as a deliberate attack and immediately responded, "Oh you are mistaken, it is Dale who got married, not me," and quickly walked away. Rowena then found Ma and told her that if she told that ridiculous marriage story one more time, she would show up at the next shindig with the biggest, blackest male friend she had, dressed in a pilot's suit, and wearing a wedding band. This was the 60s, and this sort of racial prejudice was still rampant among the people we knew. Ma certainly had not undergone any sort of conversion after the Evelyn fiasco. But she took Rowena's threat seriously and never traveled those friendly skies again.

Twenty-Nine

Ma could be wise in many ways. While I still lived at home, she encouraged me to bank most of my salary. I proudly saved and gladly contributed $10,000 when Sonny and I went furniture shopping for our new apartment. We were optimistic about our future and excited about living in Lynn, one block from the beach. The Atlantic Ocean would have been reward enough, but, for me, settling in the North Shore was an opportunity to flee my family's reputation and earn my own as a *baleboste* (praiseworthy homemaker). Subconsciously, I knew Ma loved the North Shore and would approve of my choice. I still saw everything through her eyes.

We continued to enjoy our connection to the dance crowd at the Cave, went on Florida and Las Vegas holidays, and formed friendships with other young married couples in the community. I played Mah Jongg one night a week, joined Jewish women's organizations, learned to cook and entertain, and wallowed in the simple pleasures of life. Somewhere along the path to ordination as the perfect housewife, I also became the queen of jello molds. No jello mold was too difficult for me to make! To my mind, the quest for perfection in the high art of housewifery might somehow provide social acceptance and yearned-for distance from my past.

Sonny and I even acquired a puppy, a yorky, named Andy. He was a difficult dog, and Sonny was not nearly as enamored of him as I was. The dog earned the lowest possible score in his obedience class, and on graduation day, his diploma was withheld because of poor performance. This irritated Sonny, and in spite of his dislike of the dog, he puffed up into his most menacing self and bullied the dog trainer into giving Andy an unearned diploma. It was just one small example of the darker side of my husband's personality.

I should have known ahead of time that, in its own way, Sonny's family was as big a problem as my own. Lillian and Eddie spent every Saturday with Mel and Judy and every Sunday with us. The couple arrived at my house early and stayed late, whether or not Sonny was available, and it became my wifely responsibility to entertain and feed them until it was convenient for him to join us. Lillian made certain that she had many private discussions with her son, and it became an annoyance that she knew our finances down to the last penny. This led to her discovering that Sonny, upon my request, had changed the beneficiary of his $750 life insurance policy from his mother to me. Lillian was furious.

Despite my initial reluctance about marrying Sonny, I loved him and was devoted to the marriage. I was happy to be happy. A good part of our marital success was my ability to overlook Sonny's demanding and dark disposition. After all, I was trained to comply with the wishes of my own family.

I spend a good part of the afternoon preparing a special dinner for Sonny. I am beaming when I present my exotic chicken baked in fresh pineapple shells. Instead of complimenting me on my effort

Sonny takes one look, cruelly dumps his portion into the disposal, and bolts out of the house declaring, "I'm going to get a bologna sandwich at Mel and Murray's."

Sonny never hesitated to repeat the rumors about my family, knowing that the way to hurt me was to attack their many shortcomings. He relished his taunts and often boasted to outsiders that he had rescued me. Long before we were married and I was still in school, Ma had converted my bedroom into a den with a sleep sofa, to create more living space. Sonny reinterpreted this as a callous act by Ma and often shouted that it was he who finally provided me with a "real bed." Whether it was in self defense or a simple matter of Darwinian adaptation, I developed an ability to absorb Sonny's cruelty. I simply "sucked it in."

We had been married about a year when I sensed a major change in my psychological outlook. I could not articulate what was wrong with me, but apparently, a mild depression had reared its ugly head. Rowena came to my rescue and suggested I visit her psychiatrist's colleague. Since in those days, psychotherapy was seen by many as a stigma, going to a "shrink" took all the courage I could muster, and I was too ashamed to tell anyone about it except Rowena and Sonny. Mercifully, he chose not to criticize me, because there was little doubt that I needed some help.

At the age of twenty-three, therapy was a big step for me. I had never uttered a word to a living soul, other than Rowena, about the truth of my childhood. But now I felt myself unfurling in a number of ways. I worked with my psychiatrist, slowly at first, but then the mix of pain and confusion came pouring out of me, and I didn't even try to stop it. I was finally weeping for my lost childhood, for the many injustices that Ma had handed me, and for my inability to overcome her influence. Helplessly swept along in that noisy torrent of emotion, I suddenly heard myself saying that I did not want to have children, afraid I would not be a good mother. My psychiatrist helped me understand that with a mother like Ma, my reaction was not surprising. I trusted her and considered her a valuable mentor. And so, with the guidance to systematically work through my reservations and fears, I was ultimately spared a future without the joy and fulfillment of children. I was further assured that with her unfailing professionalism, I would have the support I needed while engaging in what was to become a seemingly endless struggle with a host of trials and tribulations.

Thirty

Sonny's salary was modest, but I was grateful for what we had. He tried driving a taxi a few evenings a week to supplement his earnings as a salesman, but doing so did not suit his personality, and he quickly terminated that experiment.

He wanted nothing more than to be free of his daily insulin injections. He perceived himself as not being a whole person since he was dependent on a needle to sustain his life. He sublimated his frustration with new dreams of owning investment properties and becoming a "player." We took a real estate course together and obtained our brokers' licenses.

When a 4-unit property in the picturesque coastal community of Marblehead became available, he asked Bobby, his good friend from Malden, to go into partnership with him. Bobby brought in a money-man from Chelsea named Boobie who provided the down payment. Since Sonny had no funds to invest, his contribution was to oversee the day-to-day operations. As the lawyer of the group, Bobby provided the legal work. All three men were equal partners. Sonny was thrilled.

Sonny and I found a two-family house for sale in Swampscott, a beautiful and tranquil seaside community.

The house was sorely neglected and required multiple repairs and much renovation. But we were undaunted by the challenges and planned for the tenant's rent to help us with the mortgage. We were homeowners now.

I became pregnant. Marriage and pregnancy altered my emotional link with Ma and had the effect of shifting the balance of power a bit. I had achieved "respectability," and deluded myself into thinking my family could eschew their deviant behavior and rise to the occasion. To give her credit, Ma was generous in her gifts of household accessories, furnishings, and decorations for the baby's room.

Our son, Dean, was born in 1967, and no mother could have felt more joy and happiness. We settled in and Sonny showed a real gentleness towards his son. In fact, both our families were also bewitched by our fabulous child. Andy, our high strung dog, was not, however. He became listless and stopped eating. After a comprehensive examination, the vet diagnosed him with a serious case of jealousy and recommended offering Andy some baby food while I fed Dean. The dog responded positively and came back into the fold.

Dean was two-years-old when I became pregnant again. But three months into my pregnancy, in the middle of the night on Christmas Eve, I had a miscarriage and woke up to discover that the bed was covered in blood. Frantic, I woke Sonny to take me to the hospital. But he wanted to keep sleeping and refused, insisting that I should not bother the doctor until the morning. I cried until Sonny finally gave in. But, his initial reluctance to attend to my needs opened the door to an unpleasant emotion in me—growing resentment of his selfishness and sense of entitlement. For the first time, I saw clearly that my concerns and fears meant little to him.

After my D & C, a staff doctor came to chart the family's medical history and I felt compelled to disclose Sonny's diabetes. Extremely frightened that Sonny would be very angry, I was remorseful, like a little girl, when I admitted that I had revealed his secret. Thankfully he did not lash out at me in response.

Soon Sonny found another property to add to the first investment in Marblehead, and together, he and Boobie bought out Bobby's share of the partnership. After that, Sonny was eager to make more acquisitions, and within a few years, the partners owned five properties in Swampscott and Marblehead. Sonny was the perfect landlord, interacting with the twenty-two tenants and making whatever minor repairs he could. Boobie, eccentric but shrewd, did not care to know anything other than the monetary return on his investment. I was happy to step up as the other half of Sonny's team, and took over the job of renting the apartments and arranging for various services the tenants might require.

When Dean was three years old, I became pregnant again. I was ecstatic that the new baby was a girl—Randee.

Our future looked rosy. Sonny was the boss, and I was "the little woman," attending to the family, our house, and our real estate projects. Dean and Randee were thriving, we had good relationships with our neighbors, and I was congratulating myself because I was "making it" for the first time. My fulfillment encouraged me to try to amend missed opportunities in my youth. I enrolled in evening classes attempting to earn the elusive college degree. I became a bit of an equestrian, taking riding and jumping lessons, and a pretty good tennis player.

Thirty-One

Changes were happening all around me. As my own nurturing motherly role evolved, I began to examine the very notion of maternal love. How was it that Ma appeared to have little regard for me as a child? Why had she included Rowena and me in her sordid extracurricular life? While searching for answers, I felt that I was seeing her for the first time through adult eyes, and it was not a pretty picture. On the other hand, I knew that Ma certainly was not evil. I told myself that perhaps she did things she thought she had to do. After all, she had put food on our table and, according to her own account, rescued us from deprivation. She was a survivor, and maybe she had paid the biggest price of all in order to survive. Or had she? I couldn't be certain.

Despite my attempts to find legitimate rationalizations for Ma's shortcomings, it was hard to forgive her for what she had done to me, to Rowena, and to Daddy. Her continued intrigues and control over me pushed me to the wall. Tensions between us escalated. I wanted to hate her and make her pay for her previous behavior—for the damage she had done—and we began to have some stunning brawls. Those were not just shouting matches; they were hair-pulling, slapping, knock-down, drag-out fights.

Rowena came back into my life after years of limited contact. I was excited that she was going to live in Swampscott with her partner. As close as our emotional ties were as children, my sister and I never really had the benefit of spending enough casual time together as adults. Now we could walk to one another's houses.

She was making careful forays back into our family circle; but still struggled with the reminders of her past. I understood that she found only enough strength and motivation to cautiously dip in and out of our lives.

After thirty-five years at 1333 Blue Hill Avenue, Ma and Daddy reluctantly followed the white exodus out of Mattapan when the first floor apartment in Auntie and Bob's two-family house in Revere became available. Auntie and Ma were living in close proximity and could see each other constantly. When Dennis was fifteen, Bob threw him out of the house because the two of them were not getting along. Ma and Daddy immediately invited Dennis to move in with them, thus enabling Auntie to see her son daily.

When Mucky was no longer able to live independently, and Dennis was no longer living in the Revere house, she moved in with Ma and Daddy. Ma liked Mucky, but the offer to let her move in was not entirely altruistic. Mucky contributed her Social Security to the household economy. But that wasn't quite enough to satisfy Ma who got her hands on the key to Mucky's safety deposit box, forged Mucky's signature and helped herself to the contents. After all, Ma could never resist a little larceny, even against her own family members. Not surprisingly, this would not be the last time Ma stole from family, but I never dreamed that it would eventually happen to me. I guess I was naively wedded to the notion that I was special to Ma.

It was Rowena, with her kind nature, who ultimately became Mucky's advocate and caretaker when—with rapidly failing eyesight—she had to go to a nursing home for her last years. She had bequeathed her set of beloved holiday dishes to Rowena, but, when Mucky died, my sister never received the gift because Ma had already sold them!

My guilty feelings and the concern that I was somehow destined to become everything I disliked in my mother finally came to a head one day when she told my kids they could not have Fudgicles, because she did not want to look for them and mess up the freezer, since she was expecting guests later in the day. It was a small freezer attached to the refrigerator, not requiring much effort to sort through. On a rational level, I knew Ma loved my children. The importance placed on the anticipated visitors and seeing this kind of callousness stirred my petulance. Infuriated, I lost control and stormed out of the house, screaming at Ma, Daddy, and Auntie, resolving never to speak to them again.

Two months later, Ma and Daddy slyly told Rowena that they had just received a windfall from a stock sale. But it was one of their set-ups. They probably expected that Rowena would tell me the news and I would come crawling back to them, not wanting to miss out on a financial handout. When Rowena realized that she was being used as the pawn in their game, she, too, became infuriated. Such games and scams would never end for Ma, and Daddy added his own negative, spiteful emotions to the bubbling cauldron.

**Foxy (Dale)
High School**

**Dale, Sonny
Wedding**

**Daddy, Ma, Billy, Dale, Sonny,
& Stolen Cadillac
After Ceremony**

Part Three

Humpty Dumpty sat on a wall.
Humpty Dumpty had a great fall.
All the king's horses and all the king's men,
Couldn't put Humpty together again.

Thirty-Two

It is two o'clock on a Sunday morning in August when I am awakened suddenly out of a deep sleep by a raging whirlwind. Sonny is thrashing around in our bed, his arms and legs flailing helplessly. Then, as quickly the chaos began, he suddenly slumps back on the pillow.

He regained consciousness in the emergency room and was diagnosed with a seizure. Over the next several weeks, Sonny and I were back and forth to the Massachusetts General Hospital for a regimen of grueling tests. One required that he remained awake for twenty-four hours prior, to insure he'd sleep during the brain scan. I was his partner who made sure he stayed awake and my game plan was to keep us productive. We went apple picking with the kids during the day and had friends in for the evening. At bedtime, we peeled and sliced apples, then baked pies and cakes throughout the night. Once we depleted the cache of apples we polished the dining room chandelier. We successfully fought sleep and left for the hospital in the morning.

The kids were playing and I was about to shower when the neurologist called to say all the tests indicated that Sonny had a walnut-size calcification on his brain and required surgery. Sonny was at work, so I blithered questions into the telephone to gather as much information as possible. I hung up and calmly returned to shaving my legs when an icy reality settled upon me. Oh my G-d, I realized I would be the one to break the news to Sonny. My heart sank even further with the weight of the ominous adversary we faced.

We tried so hard to pretend our lives hadn't changed. But we had already lost control and were about to be pitched into the maelstrom of the medical system with Sonny's battery of doctors and all the comprehensive exams that would determine his surgical procedure. Something as simple as his allergy to shellfish brought its own complications because of the iodine in the dye, but the major culprit was his diabetes which presented yet another set of criteria needing serious consideration. While the medical staff strategized, I wept my fears into my pillow each night.

My life was in freefall again and nothing was happening the way it should. It had been more than a year of not speaking since Ma, Daddy and I had gone to war over the ridiculous Fudgicle incident and their attempt to lure me back through their windfall profits scam.

Lillian called every day to see if I was taking proper care of her son. When we got together, she usually found a way to remind me that I was not really a part of her family. I recall having dinner in a restaurant when she commanded me to sit at a separate table to feed baby Randee who was being fussy. It was clear that she didn't want Sonny's dinner disturbed by the bothersome noises of his infant daughter. This event dredged up a strange and lonely feeling, one that would return time and time again during Sonny's illness.

Desperate to find some moral support amidst such a barren wasteland, I contacted the local rabbi, who had recently moved to Marblehead to assume a new pulpit. Ironically, this was the same rabbi that owned the garage in Mattapan where Billy had hidden his stolen car collection several years before. The rabbi still remembered me from the old neighborhood. Even with my outlandish and unmentionable connection to him, I felt comfortable seeking his guidance. I wanted G-d to know what was happening to my family and hear my pleas for Sonny's well-being. The rabbi assured me that G-d was everywhere and would hear me wherever I was. He said I probably had other demands on my time and should not worry about *shul* (synagogue).

However, on the day of Sonny's surgery, I took six year old Dean to the synagogue and we recited our prayers with the early morning worshippers. As not-so-observant Jews, we were completely out of step with the ritual every other worshipper knew, but I had faith that G-d would recognize our sincerity in pleading for Sonny.

Lillian, Eddie, and I waited hours at the hospital for the results. Hearing the neurosurgeon say that Sonny had an inoperable Astrocytoma, a grade IV cancerous brain tumor, triggered the panic I was suppressing. His prognosis of two months to two years threw me to the floor. I started screaming hysterically. Rowena was called who in turn immediately contacted my psychiatrist. I was taken to Sonny's empty room and with my psychiatrist on the phone and, Lillian and Eddie watching helplessly, I finally settled down.

We never connected Sonny's occasional split-second thumb and index finger spasms as a precursor of a nightmare. He was 38 years old, too young, and vital for the death sentence he received. We were married only 8 years and I, with two babies, was facing widowhood at 30.

For the next six weeks, I spent every day and night at the hospital. In a daze I barely remember, I'd bring a sandwich and a cup of tea and crawl into Sonny's bed to rest beside him. I had no appetite and rapidly lost 35 pounds as I balanced the familiar cycle of our children's lives, school, Halloween, birthday parties, and play dates – with the inexorable exhausting hospital visits.

Sonny would not acknowledge his illness and often berated me when I couldn't hide my concern about his condition. This was an early sign of the wedge his non-acceptance and belligerence would soon drive between us. Lillian told Sonny only what he wanted to hear, and enabled his denial by automatically denigrating all the doctors' reports. I understood that this was his family's version of stoicism, but it seemed to me that I was no longer communicating with rational or sane people.

When Sonny was sent home, we entered the endless and debilitating routine of radiation and chemotherapy. He became a medical minefield. His gums and teeth deteriorated, his diabetes became erratic and difficult to regulate, he suffered electrolyte imbalances and frequent headaches, and his recurrent mood swings left him depressed. A once-handsome guy, he was now a scary-looking apparition with a massive scar reaching across his bald scalp from ear to ear. Inexplicably, I cut my hair very close to my scalp in a kind of burr cut, a look that caused many a stranger to stare openly. This was not a familiar style at the time, and people were either shocked by it, or admired its uniqueness. With our strange appearance, we were now a surreal duo.

More troublesome than his ruined physical appearance was Sonny's sudden impotence, at age thirty-eight. This development was a massive assault on his notion of manhood and he was outraged when the doctors named his diabetes as the culprit. However, he insisted that his condition was my fault. Because I loved him, I turned myself inside out trying to help him, but my failure to solve the problem simply fanned the flames of his growing resentment and blame.

Sonny's refusal to accept his illness was becoming an unmanageable opponent for me. Because of his unpredictable seizures, he had been told not to drive a car. But two months into his recuperation, he treated the doctors' mandate as a joke and began driving again. His arrogance allowed my arguments no more credence than those of his doctors, which added one more layer to my strife. Although I worried that his presence behind the wheel was a threat to the safety of strangers, I confess that my immediate concern was to protect my own children. So I made him promise that he would never drive our children anywhere, even if it was just around the corner for an ice cream cone. As I became both his warden and the family chauffeur, he and Lillian ridiculed me cruelly for my concern and "over-protectiveness." Then the unthinkable happened—Sonny broke his promise to me and took Lillian and the kids for a ride. Worry and constant vigilance on my part was now displaced by outright resentment and fear. That was my kids' lives they were gambling with!

Thirty-Three

Losing my husband is trial enough, but G-d, between you and me, don't even think of snatching my children from me.

One day I noticed a lump on Dean's foot and became terrified that we were on the threshold of another medical nightmare. Sonny showed no concern, not because he didn't love Dean, but because he was now solely focused on himself. That was when I realized, that somewhere along the way, he had cast off our partnership and his role as a father. As for me, I barely had enough strength to work through the doubts and confusions of another maze of doctors and another hospital as they tried to figure out what it might be. Thankfully, though, they operated on him and found only a non-malignant growth.

As if that incident was not enough to get my anxieties into overdrive, another one came soon thereafter when my friend, Laura, offered to take Randee for a play date with her daughter while I took Sonny to a medical appointment. While she was driving the car, the back door suddenly flew open and my little girl fell out of the car onto the road. This was in the days before seatbelts were taken seriously and well before the first state-mandated seatbelt law. Mercifully, there was no traffic, and Randee received only a few cuts and bruises and lost her front tooth. I was badly shaken and wondered what new and horrible disaster might befall us next.

A few weeks later, my father-in-law died of heart failure in his sleep. Eddie was a kind and amiable man and I was genuinely sad at his passing.

Fortunately, I discovered that my built-up tensions and overworked fight-or-flight reflex could be relieved by taking long walks each day. I put a leash on Andy and walked and walked and walked along the long expanse of sidewalk that borders the sea in Swampscott.

The absence of Ma and Daddy was another problem amid the turmoil. But Rowena became my life preserver, and the only family member I could actually rely upon. She kept Ma and Daddy informed of the dramatic events of my life, but still they stayed away. Were they simply being childish? Was this just another arena for one of Daddy's fits of pique? Or was Ma afraid that my needs would require more of her time than she was willing to give? I simply did not know, but I suspected that all of these things together led to the continued estrangement.

Even though Sonny was informed of his prognosis after the surgery, during one particular doctor's visit, his physician candidly told him, "Get your papers in order; you have less than a year to live." He then turned to me and said, "I hope you have a boyfriend." The second comment, delivered so shockingly in front of my sick husband, almost overshadowed the starkness of the first declaration. I was badly shaken and disarmed by the doctor's remarks. But Sonny was not outwardly bothered by either comment. As we walked to the hospital elevator, he simply told me that the doctor and I were both crazy—he was going to be just fine.

It was time for a reality check. I asked myself, how were we going to survive when Sonny was gone? Despite understanding Sonny's denial, I was very hurt when he refused to discuss the "what ifs" and make decisions for our welfare. He treated me like I was an enemy poisoning his food.

In an attempt to do some pre-planning, and wanting to avoid probate issues and a potentially contentious relationship with Boobie, I cautiously suggested to Sonny that he transfer the joint ownership of our home and investment properties to my name only. After much haranguing, Sonny agreed. But when the lawyer brought the paper work to our house, he refused to sign. I gritted my teeth and came out fighting, threatened to leave him, and thus embarrassed myself in front of the attorney. But in light of my objections, Sonny did begrudgingly sign the papers. Thereafter, there was hardly a day that he didn't accuse me of stealing his properties and insisted that I give them back. This was a new, uglier attitude than I had seen before, and the rivulet of my growing resentment gathered even more momentum and soon became a torrent. After all, I was not running away with our house and the properties on my back. I only wanted to protect my family the best way I could.

My mother-in-law, with her distinctive selfishness, requested that Sonny reinstate her as beneficiary of the $750 life insurance policy she bought when he was a child. My reaction to such an outlandish demand served to squelch any love and respect I had for her. Years later—a repeat performance—when she asked Dean and Randee to return $1000 worth of Israel bonds she had given them each as babies, they dutifully signed them back to her.

Sonny soon withdrew to the darkness of our bedroom, sometimes to nurse a headache or nausea, and at other times, to sleep or quietly listen to the radio. He had nothing of himself to give us during these times. I grieved for the loss of the "marshmallow" life I had hoped for all of us. I had two little kids who needed to flourish. I was glad to take them to the movies, the theater, or anywhere there were lights, music, and laughter. They were so sweet and good and we were each others' companions.

Perhaps I should have honored Sonny's need for solitude, but the children needed a father—at least while he was alive—and I did not always comply with his wish to be alone. I wanted him to stay involved. So, as soon as he was recovered from his surgery and treatments, I planned a trip to Disney World so the kids would have the memory of that time with their father. Sonny had little interest in this trip, but at least he was cooperative and did not ridicule my efforts.

On Sundays, I often took him and the children on family excursions, and continued to arrange play dates for the kids and dinner parties for us so that our household was at least temporarily vibrant and healthy. I was desperate to make it all feel good. But the attempts to infuse merriment into our daily lives had its price. I was exhausted, and self-pity seeped into my consciousness.

While Sonny is undergoing one of his hospitalizations for a setback, I receive an invitation to a dinner party at a friend's house. Two days before the party, Sonny is unexpectedly released from the hospital. I enthusiastically call her to say that now both of us can attend. I am shocked as she tells me not to come since his presence could upset the other guests.

Slowly, one at a time, our friends drifted away from the melancholy.

Eventually, Sonny became convinced that he was ready to go back to work. He bought a wig to wear because he did not want to publicize his illness and I did not have the heart to tell him how awful it looked. He was pleased that his boss welcomed him back. He intentionally did not reveal his prognosis and the doctor's prohibition on driving. I didn't interfere or try to squash any pleasure or hope he could glean by returning to some semblance of normalcy.

Thirty-Four

A year passes since Sonny's diagnosis. The whispers and well-intentioned sympathy of others toss me back to those childhood memories of times when I feel like an outcast. I flee to the safest places I know — isolation and distance.

I waited for the "big boom" even though Sonny worked and functioned fairly well. Miraculously, he seemed to be confounding his grim prognosis. As his caretaker, I was on twenty-four hour alert, trying to anticipate his feelings and his need for comfort and dignity. For me there was no respite. It was a tightrope act because I couldn't escape the reality which wrenched within my heart. I stopped striving to be a housewife extraordinaire and the jello molds became a thing of the past.

At the age of 31, I found that the dose of harsh reality which had entered my life had toughened me up and enabled me to focus on only the most important things. I could have gone back to work as a legal secretary or a real estate broker and probably should have, because we certainly could have used the money. Instead, I inexplicably decided to become a nurse, a process which would take several years, during which the earning power I already had would be lost. Why did I make this decision? Maybe I rationalized subconsciously that the nobility of nursing would remove some of the stain from my family's reputation. Maybe I thought that as a professional, I would be better able to support my children in the long run. Or, maybe, as my psychiatrist suggested, I harbored the subconscious notion that, as a registered nurse, I could somehow help Sonny survive his illness. I have no idea of the actual reasons. I only know that I made it without realizing that the demanding nursing curriculum was definitely not designed for a mother of two young children who was preparing herself for widowhood.

Nevertheless, I geared up for the required SAT exams by engaging the top math student at Swampscott High to tutor me in algebra and geometry. But I was quickly overwhelmed while watching her whiz through the test exercises, and decided not to meet with her again. How I managed to get an acceptable score in the SATs without any tutoring is a complete mystery to this day. But with the SATs out of the way, I now faced the granddaddy of all courses, Organic Chemistry. I gritted my teeth and dragged myself through the lectures and laboratories at Salem State College. That experience alone should have snapped me out of my delirium, but I was intensely driven by the desire to become a nurse and did not entertain the notion of failure.

After passing the course, I arranged for a tuition loan and chose the three- year program at Lynn Hospital because it was only 20 minutes away and the least expensive of the available alternatives. To most young people, the commitment to get a nursing degree is all-consuming. But for me—a person whose life was crowded with other important commitments—it actually provided an escape from my problems and brought a measure of balance into my life. The kids' safety and activities were constantly on my mind. Besides school, I made detailed arrangements to ensure their days were fulfilling. In order for me to succeed, all that planning had to go smoothly. For the most part, it did.

Going to school was exciting because I had a love of learning. It made me feel alive, and to keep that feeling going, I went through my daily routine with near-military precision so that other things did not take over and crowd out my school life. My mornings started at 5 AM when I dressed, walked Andy, and then awoke the kids to prepare them for the day. I was then out the door by 6:15. Sonny stayed with the kids until their school day began. After my classes, I picked them up from their after-school activities, prepared dinner, cleaned up, bathed them, and had them ready for bed by seven. Then I studied until midnight and repeated the routine the next day, and the next day, and the next. On weekends I caught up on chores around the house and studied. My generalized sorrow about Sonny combined with this high level of frenetic activity produced an emotional numbness that felt just right to me.

After the first semester, Sonny had a serious relapse, was hospitalized, and then recovered. I postponed enrollment in the second semester to take care of him. During that time, we engaged in birthday celebrations, play dates and other displays of apparent normalcy, but behind the façade, Sonny was torturing me relentlessly about his impotence. It had been two years since we successfully had sex. His endocrinologist suggested an implant but Sonny never followed through. As far as he was concerned, his impotence was still my fault. He was self-absorbed and insensitive. I resented his inability to be kind and acknowledge my love and support. I was in a prison with no escape.

It was morbid in the house, lacking in laughter and joy. I turned to food for comfort. I often ate an entire pizza and consumed ice cream by the carton as the tears flowed. I put on twenty five pounds. As a child, I felt isolated and ashamed and often ate to mask those feelings. Now I was eating to banish a flood of loneliness and despair.

The brightness of my children's faces was my only salvation. They, all too well, understood their father was sick and assumed much more responsibility than two little kids should shoulder. I ached for their loss of innocence. We were forming the armor of "us against the world."

Thirty-Five

What is the color of gloom? It takes shape in so many ways but cannot be seen. It sucks out the energy of our once thriving household, replacing it with silence and washing away whatever comfort we manage to scrape together. The air is stale from the absence of fresh flowers or open windows. Can a mother's touch be as loving to her children if no one is reaching out to touch the mother?

Sonny's losses were piling up faster than ever. He developed retinopathy, a result of his diabetes, and after undergoing several unsuccessful laser treatments, he was declared blind in one eye and could no longer work.

One evening, while our children slept, his boss came to the house to retrieve the company vehicle assigned to him. The three of us engaged in polite chatter, but I had to turn away when Sonny signed the termination papers. I knew that, with this simple act, he was relinquishing the last vestige of his dignity—the ability to work—and I was distraught. Sonny, on the other hand, seemed strangely composed. I cried and cried for both of us.

He had no job, no salary, no sex, and no future. I wondered how much more the man could reasonably endure. His disability payments ended, and we were left with Social Security Assistance and the upstairs tenant's rent as our only income sources. With $7,000 in savings and our investment properties not yet generating profit, there simply was no extra money.

Ma had handled the problem of impending poverty in her own unique way, and Rowena and I suffered mightily for it. Now it was my turn to figure out how to run a household in which the father was unable to support his family. The past was now biting me in the ass. Ma and Daddy's machinations made me well aware of being careful with money, but these circumstances propelled me into a hyper vigilance that I would never outgrow.

I found myself thinking more and more about Ma. She would not have allowed herself or me to succumb to defeat and would have said, "You have your own life and the kids' lives to account for. You have the strength and cannot wait for people to help you. Never mind what people say because they always have a lot to say. Courage, my dear."

I kept on digging deeper and deeper to stay mentally tough and was determined to save my children and myself. The possibility of the kids being left behind the other children, in our affluent and goal-oriented community, was the motivation for my seeking financial assistance for Hebrew School and Temple membership. The kids also received scholarships from Jewish Family Services for a month of summer camp.

Then there were the troublemakers, like the local optometrist, who lacked compassion for our financial situation. After examining Dean's eyes, he became incensed when I produced two pairs of eyeglass frames my Uncle Bob sold me at cost. He then reported my uncle to his employer without regard for the consequences. He was only interested in his lost revenue rather than my difficult circumstances.

Now I was frightened about the present and terrified for our future. Sonny had exceeded all expectations. Two and a half years beyond his death sentence, we were still hanging in there. I wondered if the doctors were mistaken. I was filled with remorse for even thinking about the calendar.

It seems to me that the reason doctors estimate life expectancy is because loved ones want to be able to ration their energies and be available for the patient at the end. And maybe, just maybe, families need to know when their own lives can begin again.

Questions pounded in my head. Were the kids getting enough love and attention? Were they worried and depressed about their father? I contacted the Big Brother and Big Sister organizations, hoping that additional support would be beneficial. For a year or so, Randee's big sister came to the house every couple of weeks to play with her. But Dean refused any relationship with his big brother. I could only guess that he felt warming up to a surrogate was a betrayal of his father.

Nice families help one another. I did not expect much from my own family, but I certainly expected more than we were getting from Sonny's. So, I met with Mel and Judy, without Sonny's knowledge, and pleaded with them to help us by being more supportive. They had been attentive after Sonny's surgery, but when there were so many emergencies, the crises became a status quo and their attentions faded away. I could not blame them—I, too, wanted to get away from the situation—and could see that they did not have the conscience, time, or inclination to try any harder. Was an occasional trip to the ice cream parlor or a ride for Sonny and the kids too much to ask? We needed them and some TLC but none was forthcoming.

Not surprisingly, Rowena—who knew so well what it was like to be alone and without help—provided me some of the support I needed. We spoke by phone several times a-day, and just hearing her concerned voice had a calming effect on me, even when I was reacting irrationally. One day I called her sobbing because I had just burned a batch of brownies. She kindly explained that the brownies were not really the issue. I worried that my calls for help were a serious drain on her time and efficiency at work, but she did not complain.

Finally, after more than two years of no communication with Ma and Daddy, I gave in and called. I needed to hear their voices and feel closer to them. To my surprise, it was as though we had never been estranged. Just speaking to them was a magical elixir. Daddy encouraged me to leave Sonny and not waste any more years. I told him I wasn't going anywhere, but I did appreciate what he said—callous as it may have seemed—because I knew it was an expression of his regard for me.

After this reconciliation, Daddy and Ma were vacation-ing in the Catskills when Daddy suffered a massive heart attack. Rowena and I immediately drove to where they were, not at all certain that he would be alive when we got there. Despite his indifferent performance as a father, we loved him and wanted to be with him. His brothers also drove up to see him, perhaps for the last time. Becky later made the long trip on several subsequent weekends and sat at Daddy's bedside. Their rift, at the Passover Seder, years before had finally dissolved and the two found meaning and closeness in those visits.

Daddy recovered and the gift of continued life brought about an amazing change in him. He was finally taking care of himself. He got involved. He became communicative—even lively—and he even quit smoking 3-5 packs of Camels a day. Time was running out for Becky, however. He died at the age of 60 while sitting at the beach in his car.

Ma and Daddy started to invite me out with them on weekends. He was in one of his upbeat periods, and Ma had been successful in getting him to clean up, dress up, and go out dancing with her. These were the days of the disco scene, and the three of us blew off steam with our frenetic dancing to the music of the Bee Gees, Donna Summer, The Jacksons and more. Once again, we were a family; I was them and they were me. Life at home would remain the same, but, like Daddy with his unpredictable ups and downs, I was oddly re-energized for a time.

Thirty-Six

I am enjoying a late fall bike ride when Alex, a casual tennis acquaintance, stops his car to say hello to me and chat. During our conversation, he reveals that his wife has a mental illness and has endured several hospitalizations. She has been stable for a while, but is like a fragile child. He laments the loss of adult companionship in his life, and then flirtatiously invites me to go on his next business trip to Spain. Of course, that is out of the question, but I am excited by this escalation of our friendship, and we agree to meet for dinner, knowing full well that there is a mutual attraction. G-d knows, I crave affection and tenderness in my life.

Infidelity was a subject I knew a lot about. I understood what it could do to a family and had always told myself I would live my life on the straight and narrow. But my tightly woven design for the future had never included the wild threads of impending death and desolation that were beginning to infiltrate and destroy my plan.

Sonny had long ago stopped being considerate of me and so I told myself I needed some caring male companionship to maintain my sanity. I recognized the opportunity Alex's dinner invitation offered, and rationalized that accepting it was directed at my emotional survival, not promiscuity. Neither one of us was interested in hurting or abandoning our ailing partners but only to refill each other's depleted reservoirs. But the dinner was just the start of our relationship. To avoid being seen by the locals, we soon began getting together for early morning tennis matches at his club, or for brisk walks and bike rides. We had quiet dinners at dusk and shared tenderness and intimacy in the stolen hours we had together. In the process, his kindness and intelligence bolstered my collapsing spirit.

When spring came, I started thinking about returning to nursing school to complete my interrupted first year. It would have been so much easier to just forget about this particular dream. Attending school had become my version of the Holy Grail. Sonny said he certainly did not want me to abandon the program in order to stay home with him. He was eligible for an SSI visiting aide four hours a day and knew that the aide could help him with whatever he wanted. In addition, he had the buddy system of men friends I had organized to take him to lunch several days a week. Lillian was also available to spend time with him whenever he was alone. I was beholden to all of them for their care and compassion.

To others, I may have seemed outwardly calm and rational, but inside, my emotions were in turmoil and I was not always sane. This became painfully clear when I was getting ready for school one morning in my darkened living room. I unexpectedly stepped on several warm piles of Andy's poop and reacted hysterically. The poor little dog was having digestive problems, but we could not afford to pay for the vet to treat him and continued to deal with his condition ourselves. But this particular accident somehow became the final straw for me. I know I was not in my right mind when I told Sonny to go with his aide that day and take my beloved Andy to the vet to be put down.

Three years passed since Sonny's diagnosis when he suddenly lost sight in his other eye. He was now totally blind. It was terrifying to watch him bumping into walls, and screaming and pounding them with his fists out of sheer frustration. He was like a lion growling and ferociously trying to break out of his cage. I grieved silently for him as I fed him, describing the location of each type of food on the plate as: "Twelve o'clock—potatoes, three o'clock—peas, six o'clock—meat." Tear-jerking, heartbreaking and pitiful...take your pick...any one of them describe what we were all living through.

Carroll Center for the Blind in Newton offered a two-week program to determine a blind person's suitability for their three-month residential training course intended to teach blind people to perform daily living skills. Sonny enrolled in the evaluation program with the expectation of getting a chance to learn some level of independence.

I am downtown Boston when I spot Sonny with a group of other blind people from the Center and watch as the instructor guides the group through the crowds to a nearby concert. Seeing my tough guy husband looking so meek and helpless makes the blood rush to my head and drowns out the street noises. Despite all that has happened to our relationship while we endured the privations of his disease, my heart feels as if it is being ripped from its moorings. Oh Sonny, my poor husband!

Not surprisingly, Sonny was deemed an unsuitable candidate for the residential program, possibly because of his steady resistance to the help they were offering him. But the Carroll Center did provide an instructor to come to the house and teach him to use a cane and other aids.

He had long since lost interest in the day-to-day management of the properties and relied on me to monitor the tenants, arrange for maintenance, and provide the bookkeeping. I also began to get involved in our personal finances. It was then that I noticed the Social Security check we received—which was always directly deposited to the bank—paid out more than Sonny had indicated to me. When I questioned him about the discrepancy, he admitted that he had lied so that he could have extra money for himself. I was hurt by the betrayal but familiar with this kind of selfishness—I had certainly seen a lot of it in Ma— and I began to worry that he might irrationally decide to dip into our $7000 worth of savings. In order to protect my family, I placed that money in an account that only I could control. When I told him what I had done, the information opened another emotional divide between us.

I think Sonny now felt that he had finally lost all control over his own life, but he didn't lose the ability to be vindictive. His descent into blindness was grim for all of us, but now he was more cantankerous and difficult as each day passed, making him almost impossible to deal with. He taunted me unmercifully about stealing his properties and his house. I held my temper but wanted to scream. He began to confuse the kids by telling them that when I was occasionally out, socially with friends, it was because I did not want to be home with them.

I had tucked away a $100 bill with some singles in a purse for use in an emergency. One day when I looked in the purse, I noticed that the bill was gone and worried that I had spent it, mistaking it for a $1 bill. I anguished about my apparent carelessness and regretted the loss of that much money when we needed it so badly. But months later, from the backseat of the car, a teary Dean suddenly blurted out that Sonny ordered him to take the $100 bill and give it to him. This heartless manipulation of his own child was one of the lowest points in the saga of Sonny's plunge into his personal version of Hell on earth. To this day, I keep tucked away a $100 bill in the same small black purse as a reminder of my vulnerability.

By now, the physical and emotional demands of our family nightmare had spread me so thin that I could no longer continue the relationship with Alex. So I said goodbye to him and to that little island of tenderness and caring that we had established for ourselves.

Many years later, I find myself in Alex's old house for a festive dinner party in Swampscott. He has long since moved out, and the new owners have become recent friends of mine. As I walk into the familiar sunroom to pick up a drink at the bar, I smile inwardly as I remember him fondly.

Thirty-Seven

I had the first year of nursing school under my belt and the kids were again awarded a month at overnight camp. While they were away, Sonny and I spent the days together, often at Marblehead Harbor where we sat on a bench and I narrated for him the activities going on around us. I attempted to paint a picture of the fishermen as they hauled in their catches while the sea birds hovered, hoping to grab whatever slipped through the nets. I described the tourists as they wandered around the streets, taking photographs and eating ice cream cones. I read to him while he enjoyed a snack in the fresh air. This simple routine became a favorite refuge for us, and the memories of it are a source of calm amidst the many turbulent and traumatic reminders of those years.

That summer, I met a sophisticated, outgoing, and debonair Englishman named Ed. He was tall and thin, with dark, attractive looks, and immaculately dressed. I was immediately struck by his charm and friendliness, and his English accent certainly took nothing away from his overall appeal. Ed explained that he had been a successful clothing manufacturer in Manchester, England. When his wife wanted to move to Australia with their three children, he sold his company with the idea of starting up a new business in Sydney. But his marriage fell apart—perhaps because of his love of the Baccarat tables and the secret girlfriend his son discovered he had. He moved to New York, where his mother and siblings were living, and took a job in the garment industry. Then Ed was offered a job as the manager of a leather factory in the adjacent town of Lynn. When I met him, he had lost that job and was bumming around for the summer. At the time, Rowena had been dating men, and so I offered to arrange a meeting for the two of them. Their rendezvous was not a success.

I bumped into Ed several times after his date with Rowena and got the clear impression that he was planning these chance encounters with me. It wasn't long before he asked me out to dinner, and from then on, it was apparent that we were not going to ignore or deny our mutual attraction.

I had endured four long years of total immersion in the slow-growing effects of Sonny's terminal illness. I was angry for the cheap shots he took at me to make himself feel manly, at his family for their inability to accept the truth about his prognosis, and that my kids' childhood was being shortchanged. I was desperately lonely. Ed saw all of this, and began to give me the kind of comfort I had sorely missed in my marriage.

When Ed met Sonny, he graciously offered to help with errands or in any other way he could. And so, by the time the kids returned from camp that summer, Ed had become a benevolent and helpful friend to both Sonny and me. To Sonny, he provided lively male companionship. To me, he quickly restored an enthusiasm for life and made me feel like the young woman I had forgotten I was. We were now fully engaged in a second generation love triangle. The trio of Sonny, Ed and me looked a whole lot like that of Daddy, Billy, and Ma.

When Ed accepted a job in Chicago, our whole family felt the loss because, in such a short period, he had become an integral part of all of our lives. But I also felt a degree of relief that my summer fling was ending because I was entering my second year of nursing school and couldn't use my valuable time for such a powerful distraction. Besides, I told myself, we still had the telephone. I remember one particularly rough period with Sonny when Ed called and I stretched out on the kitchen floor weeping hysterically while he said empathetic and reassuring things to calm me down.

Sonny's ophthalmologist suggested that he fly to Wisconsin to get some specialized eye surgery that had been developed there. If successful, the delicate procedure could at least partially restore his vision. Because school had already started for the kids and me, Lillian signed on to accompany Sonny to his surgery

After two post-operative weeks in Milwaukee, Sonny returned to Lillian's house for a month for the total bed rest and quiet required for his successful recovery. Amazingly, he regained limited sight which was further enhanced by special eyeglasses. We all cheered for him, but I found myself inwardly dreading his return to our household. It was obvious that his time away from our home had brought a sense of peace and calm that had long eluded us.

Then Sonny—always tenacious—contacted his former employer and convinced him to let him make telephone sales calls to prospective customers for a small stipend. We squeezed a desk into our bedroom, and had a special line installed–the red phone, commanding its own attention– which became his link to the sales world. He also continued his luncheon dates with friends. The combination of these activities made his days more purposeful, but that sour mood and bad disposition were always lurking just below the surface.

One snowy day, our neighbor's teenage daughter volunteered to shovel our tenant's driveway. I was in the kitchen when she was talking to Sonny at the front door about the project. Suddenly the two of them were shouting obscenities at one another, and by the time I reached the door, she had slapped him across the face and he had responded in kind. I have no idea what prompted the argument, but it didn't really matter. She had slapped a sick and dying man. I conceded that he was wrong to retaliate, but told myself he was emotionally unstable and his action should not seem surprising to anyone. I apologized to the girl and her parents for Sonny's behavior and desperately hoped that was the end of the fracas. But my apologies were not at all sufficient. The teenager's irate mother solicited the allegiance of the surrounding neighbors, and suddenly we found ourselves shunned and unwelcomed at all their activities. But life went on, regardless of this new source of discontent.

I had just completed my second year of nursing school when Ed began calling more frequently. He complained that his job was barely adequate and asked me to come to Chicago for a few days to cheer him up. With almost no hesitation, I arranged for Lillian to stay with Sonny and the kids for the weekend. I told them Rowena was going with me and asked her to back up my story. Once again, Rowena was forced into her traditional role of beard and to cover for someone else's bad behavior. But this time, I was the one doing the lying and cheating, not Ma. When I arrived in Chicago, I was overcome with remorse and left the next day.

That was *not* what Ma would have done, and I consoled myself by rationalizing that my regret was genuine and I was at least trying to rectify a very bad decision.

Soon, Ed either was fired or quit the Chicago job and took a job in New Jersey, saying he wanted to be closer to me geographically. I did not believe his declaration but his professional instability had its own rewards. He often drove to Boston to visit, and I boldly arranged with Ma to let him stay at her house while he was in town. Now Ma was covering for me! We had come full circle. Ed quit the New Jersey job after a short tenure there and began work in a coat manufacturing company in Biddeford, Maine, only an hour or so away from Boston.

After almost five years of illness, it was beginning to look as if Sonny had beaten his death sentence. I shocked and disgusted myself by occasionally speculating as to how much longer he could possibly last. I could see that our kids were losing their innocence in a household that was as distorted and dysfunctional as my own childhood home had been. I was just as powerless to prevent the situation as I had been as a child.

When the kids were gearing up for their third annual month at camp, I mustered the courage to tell Sonny that I planned to drive them to camp and then continue to Maine to visit Ed. Sonny did not object—at least not to my face—and Lillian made no overt protest about taking care of Sonny in my absence. By this time, it was clear that Sonny didn't care about me or my behavior. He was only interested in his own survival. I assuaged myself that with the kids away and having fun, there would be no one who would miss me, and Lillian would take good care of Sonny. Despite the guilt—the ever-present, nagging guilt—I somehow convinced myself that I was doing the best I could under trying circumstances.

Soon I was headed to Maine with my bike on a rack, wearing the dungaree cutoffs that would become my vacation uniform. Ed was staying in a shabby hotel room above a saloon with sagging curtains, peeling paint and a dingy kitchenette. The place was reminiscent of a slightly overdone stage set, and to add to the general seediness, we were frequently awakened at night by the smashing of bottles on the bar followed by raucous fighting. None of these details fazed me in the least. Inwardly, I was appalled at the choices I was making, but made no attempts to rectify them. Instead, I felt relieved that I had escaped my problems for the time being.

While Ed went to work, I spent the days biking to nearby hamlets, going to the beach and reading. In the evenings we went out to dinner, to a movie or to a jazz club. Then, during his vacation week, we took an exhilarating windjammer cruise out of the quaint seaport town of Camden. One weekend, Ma and Daddy even drove up to visit us. Now Ma and Daddy looked like a devoted married couple, and I looked like Ma, sneaking out with one of her boyfriends and lying through her teeth about it.

I called Sonny daily to check on his welfare, and reassured myself that since he was only an hour's drive away, I could get home quickly if needed. When camp ended, I picked up the kids and drove them straight to Ed's for a few days before going home. We all crowded into the one room and kitchenette above the bar with the shattering glass beer bottles and the fistfights. They liked Ed and enjoyed all the goofy adventures he had planned for their visit.

When I returned home, I was surprised to find that Mel and Judy had been spending time regularly with Sonny and Lillian. It was no stretch to guess that they had been talking about me. Then I found documentation indicating that

Sonny's profit-sharing trust of $15,000 had been revised. Judy was a legal secretary and had helped make the changes which indicated that I was no longer a beneficiary and Mel was now the trustee. The proceeds of the trust were to be divided between Dean and Randee when each of them turned twenty three. Mel was also appointed the executor of Sonny's will. Sonny specified that his prized diamond ring was to be given to Dean at age 23 or earlier, based upon Mel's discretion. There were no other assets.

Mel, a tormenter, later added the nasty verbal caveat that the estate would be distributed only if he was satisfied that the kids "deserved" the money. As long as the money would eventually be paid to the kids, this slap in the face was wasted on me. But the thing that rankled was Mel putting himself in a position to judge my children.

Thirty-Eight

If I had any doubts during my second year of nursing school, my third and final year was overwhelming and punishing. Three days a week, hospital rotations and instruction, 6:30AM until 3:30PM or 3:30PM until 11:30PM, plus two full days of classes, plus homework, plus, plus, plus. I loved learning but hated the demands.

I respected that Lillian loved her son and did as much for him as she possibly could. As a mother myself, I could feel her pain. But she changed the rules of engagement when she began telling me that she wished Sonny's cancer on me. One day, her epithets and cursing unnerved me so much that I reacted to a particularly aggressive onslaught like an injured snake, hissing and spitting at my tormentor to protect myself from another vicious attack. It is hard to know who was more dismayed by this primitive reaction, Lillian or me. As far as I was concerned, in my misery, I was becoming someone I didn't even recognize.

On another home front, it was upsetting to know that Daddy was rapidly deteriorating due to several attacks of congestive heart failure. I was seeing less of him and Ma— mainly for brief visits during his hospitalizations. That too was breaking my heart, but there was little I could do.

When we were offered a free suite for Christmas week in a Florida hotel through the family of Dean's best friend, I jumped at the opportunity. I borrowed money for the airfare and was pleased that our family had a chance to be in a different environment.

Unfortunately, it was cold and rained in Florida most of the time we were there, and staying indoors caused us all to become a bit frayed around the edges. One day, I was annoyed that Sonny was acting vitriolic and we began to argue. In the heat of our squabble, I lost my temper and swung at him, striking him in the chest. When he began writhing in pain, I was terrified that I might have broken his ribs. I was completely shaken and pleaded with G-d that Sonny should be alright. After the pain subsided, I was thankful that he was not injured. My reactions to stress were becoming unpredictable and uncontrollable and I castigated myself mercilessly for taking a swing at my ill husband.

There was more. Sonny's sight was failing again and he was miserable. His rage alarmed me. In view of his growing hostility, his erratic and unpredictable outbursts, I now believed that Sonny might actually try to hurt me. So I began to sleep on the living room sofa each night. I was now out of the bedroom, but still did not feel safe. I wondered obsessively if I was going to hit him again, and if he was going to kill me in retaliation. I needed peace. The speeded-up paranoid thoughts were tumbling round and round in my consciousness, and finally I made the decision to get Lillian to move into our house to care for Sonny so that the kids and I could move to one of our nearby available rental apartments.

It was a lonely and tough choice for which I felt shame. It tormented me and made me realize that my wifely resolve at the beginning of Sonny's illness—to take care of him no matter what—had completely crumbled. We had lived with his prognosis and illness for five long years. He had beaten the odds and I was happy that he was still alive, but now I was no longer willing to sacrifice my life for his. To my disordered and terrified mind, staying there with Sonny would be no less than my own death sentence. I was searching for an unqualified endorsement from within, and, of course, that was not possible. I was damned if I did and damned if I didn't. My salvation was that Lillian would stay with Sonny.

Rowena and Ma encouraged me to leave our house so that I could find immediate relief. My psychiatrist understood my anguish but warned that I would struggle mightily with oppressive guilt later on. For me, the choice came down to my need for sanity versus my husband's need for constant care by a family member. What kind of choice was this? My torment was so great that, at times, I believed it would be better for me to stay with him despite my concern about possible violence. Ultimately I was not satisfied with that solution, and continued to chastise and debate myself obsessively. In the end, I opted to move out and tried not to dwell on how shaky I felt about the decision. In a weak attempt to justify my choice, I reminded myself that Sonny had proven his durability. I did not want to abandon him; I just wanted to save my children and myself.

Our small apartment was just ten minutes away from the house. I slept on a sofa bed in the living room and Dean and Randee shared the only bedroom. The kids seemed to be doing all right even though they obviously would have preferred living in our real home. I drove them to their school when I didn't have an early hospital shift, or they walked, or they slept over at the house. We visited Sonny every day after school and did a few chores for him if he asked. I did our laundry and we all had dinner together frequently. Mel and Judy were seeing more of Sonny and Lillian, and I encouraged the kids to attend special family celebrations. But I avoided any social situations with Sonny's family, and felt like a pariah most of the time.

Thirty-Nine

Ed surfaced again. He had quit yet another job and was proposing to move in with the kids and me. It was comforting to think he would now be close because we all loved his nurturing soul and good cheer. But, mainly, I needed him emotionally and convinced myself that other people were more relaxed about their needs and decisions for personal happiness. I was separated from Sonny, albeit without legal documentation, and rationalized that the kids would survive. After all, as a child I had survived Ma's indiscretions.

As soon as I told him he could live with us, Ed began to inextricably weave himself into our lives. He participated in the kids' carpools, played with them, shopped, and more often than not, when my hospital shift ended, welcomed me with a home-cooked English-style dinner. He ironed our clothes and made curtains for the kitchen and bathroom windows. I loved him for his *Yiddishkeit* (Jewishness) and empathetic manner.

It was in this state of relative calm and contentment amidst the ruins that I finally finished three and a half grueling years of nursing school. Friends planned a graduation party with a buffet dinner. Their gesture brought me to tears because I had good reason to assume that I had become a complete social outcast.

To finally acquire a formal education was a major milestone for me. It bolstered my self-esteem and confidence. Now a bona fide Registered Nurse, I decided to pursue a path of psychiatric nursing and selected Massachusetts Mental Health Center (formerly Boston Psychopathic Hospital), a teaching hospital for Harvard. As intimidating as the wards seemed, I found them fascinating. I was assigned to the care of catatonic schizophrenics and manic depressives alike and dealt with patients who were so aggressive that the staff often had to call in security guards when we administered medical care. Alone, I escorted 12 patients on the elevator to their cafeteria meal and was always grateful that no one went berserk. Oddly enough, that chaotic, crazy world made my own messed-up existence seem benign and temperate by comparison.

I laugh at myself emulating Jack Nicholson's character in the movie, "One Flew Over the Cookoo's Nest." He organizes his fellow patients to watch a baseball game on television, so I attempt to congregate my patients in the TV room to enjoy the Macy's Thanksgiving Day Parade. When one or two finally sit, another one or two jump up and wander away. It is musical chairs. How's this for pure poetry — I lack Jack's knack.

But there was a higher order of business why I wanted to work there. That was where Rowena was court-ordered, twenty-two years previously, to inpatient observation to decide if she was crazy because she was a lesbian. I needed to re-visit and attempt to understand my sister's experience. It made me feel closer to her.

The year and a half of regained sight had been a welcome but transitory gift for Sonny. His seizures were increasing and he was now headed into total, irrevocable blindness. I was working at the hospital when Dean and Randee frantically called me to say that they had been with Sonny when he experienced a seizure. Although he came out of it quickly, they were frightened. I rushed home immediately.

Shortly thereafter, he stopped talking and responding. The doctors hypothesized that Sonny's tumor was stable and his lack of responsiveness had been brought on by brain damage caused by the diabetic seizures. Anything was possible, but it seemed to me that he had finally given up his long struggle.

Sonny was hospitalized at Mass General, fed by IVs, catheterized, and secured with a Posey restraint for his safety. The kids and I visited him frequently, always encouraging him to get better in time to attend Dean's upcoming Bar Mitzvah. But Sonny never responded and would never attend the ceremony.

From the days when I was a voyeur in Karen's house, I had become skillful at copying how "normal" people lived and acted. This attempt by mimicry was all part of the pursuit of normalcy, and of course, I wanted to do Dean's Bar Mitzvah the right way, so I would not embarrass myself or my son. When I sat down with the rabbi to go over the details of the religious ceremony and reception, I became overwhelmed with sorrow and loneliness, and found myself sobbing uncontrollably.

Dean's big day was marred by his father's absence. To help ease the pain I made a point of arranging with the rabbi that members of Sonny's family be honored with *aliyahs* (reading a Torah portion). Dean performed wonderfully on the *bimah* (raised platform with reading desk) and was happy with his achievement. After the services we had a simple dignified catered buffet luncheon at the Temple. I chose not to have the traditional music and entertainment, because it felt inappropriate in view of Sonny's situation. But that evening, we held a wild and noisy DJ party at home for the kids.

When Dean opened his Bar Mitzvah presents that evening, there was nothing from Sonny's family. The next day, Mel called to tell me that he had asked all of them to make their gift checks payable to him—a total of $298—to keep me from "squandering the money" and said he planned to save it and give it to Dean on his eighteenth birthday. Ultimately, this gesture was too crude even for Mel, and he admitted that he was embarrassed by what he had done and endorsed the checks back to Dean. My mother-in-law claimed she knew nothing of the scheme, but I did not believe her. She herself had given a check to Mel. I was so disgusted and angry about their treatment of Sonny's innocent child that instead of putting the money into his savings account, I indulged him with an Atari, one of the first video games.

Sonny remained in an uncommunicative state, and after a few months of hospitalization, Mel called to inform me that he would be making all the decisions necessary for his care and that I would no longer be involved. I did not know if he was designated as Sonny's health care proxy, or if he was just badgering me. I was in such a distraught emotional state that it was easy for Mel to bully me. It never occurred to me to ask for verification.

Mel placed Sonny in a nursing home close to Lillian's apartment so she could visit him regularly. The nursing home required a $30,000 annual private payment, guaranteed for two years, in addition to Sonny's monthly social security benefits. The extra compensation was necessary because Sonny was only 45 years old, still strong, and could potentially live many more years despite his total impairment. Although I readily agreed to sell our interest in the real estate properties to guarantee the money, Mel relished his power over me and found satisfaction in frequent threats to also take the kids away from me. Ed urged me to move back into my own house for their sake and to avoid any possible legal ramifications. Since I thought Sonny would rally and return home, my initial reaction was to resist the idea. Eventually I moved out of the apartment.

Forty

Oh, I wish I could pretty up the next part of the story, but I cannot. Christmas vacation provided a brief hiatus from school, so I planned to drive to Florida with the kids and Ed for a quick respite. A few days before leaving, I called the nursing home to check on Sonny and was informed he was in the hospital again suffering from an infection. No one notified me because Mel arranged to be the primary contact. Then I called the hospital to get a report on Sonny's health and was told they could not release that information to me. I considered canceling the trip but was not particularly alarmed since he had been hospitalized numerous times before. He had been in a non-communicative state for several months and I didn't think it mattered if I visited him at the nursing home when we returned rather than the hospital.

When we reached Miami, I called Ma to check in, and she was frantic as she told me that Sonny had died. A friend of mine had learned of his death and called her. If Lillian or Mel had tried to locate me (it was before the days of answering machines) to give me this news, they certainly never contacted my mother or Rowena. I immediately phoned Mel and he informed me coldly that all the funeral arrangements had already been made, like it or not. The kids and I flew home immediately.

Mel meant what he said about arranging Sonny's funeral. He, Lillian, Judy and their kids drove to the cemetery in a limousine while the kids and I drove in our own car. The newspaper obituary Mel supplied did not even mention that Sonny had a wife. I knew the family was getting back at me and, to a degree, I saw their point. Nevertheless, I was stung by their cruelty. Afterwards, there was a *shiva* (Jewish mourning period) at Mel's house and a separate one at mine.

In viewing the past from the vantage point of the present, I wonder what the hell was wrong with me. Why did I allow Mel to dictate the terms of my family's continued existence? Why did I let such a vindictive person threaten to take custody of my kids, manipulate me into promising to sell the properties, and plan Sonny's funeral? I had run out of strength, wasn't able to think clearly, and reacted to his power plays by curling up in a ball, hoping he wouldn't hurt me anymore.

To this day, I have not forgiven myself for being away when Sonny died. I know that it was not a malicious or uncaring act. In attempting to assuage my feelings, I am certain that Mel or Lillian wouldn't even have called us to be at Sonny's side since they didn't even inform me of his hospitalization.

When I was a kid, I always called for my mother when I fell down. No matter if she was out of earshot, that involuntary little yelp would wiggle out of me on its own. On the day of the funeral, I emitted that cry again—because I wanted my family. But Ma, although she fully understood her obligations, was unwilling to risk offering comfort and care, and in her usual way, feared that my little family would require more of her than she was willing to invest. So she went to her health club to relax before going to the funeral, and went home directly after the burial, not bothering to go to the house to support us while we were sitting *shiva*. Auntie, an inseparable piece of my life, could not find time to attend any of this and instead sent her son Dennis to represent her. Daddy, with his uncertain moods and fading resolve, did not show up at all. Thank goodness, Rowena was there to hold me up as she had so many times before.

A year later, the unveiling of Sonny's grave stone brought me together with his family again. I expected nothing unusual, and was completely caught off guard when I saw that the stone—arranged for by Mel—read simply, "Son, Brother, and Father." Where was there a mention of "Husband?" What about all those years we spent as a married couple including those years in which disaster overtook us? Was our history together to be erased by the cruelty of a younger brother? I was embarrassed in front of my own children.

Sonny had been the center of my universe, the magnet that either drew me close or repelled me. He had been ill for six and a half years. Yes, I was afraid my youth would dissipate while I met the demands of my dying husband. Yes, I was afraid my kids would miss a fair chance at their own lives. Yes, I allowed myself to become involved with other men. Yes to all of it, but the last line of the last chronicle would read that when he died, I was not there. There were no celestial trumpets for a defeated warrior. For better or worse, my husband for almost fifteen years simply slipped through a crack in the universe. I think I expected to feel some relief at the end of such a long and nightmarish siege. Instead, I felt nothing but sadness and emptiness.

Forty-One

We settled into our lives, comprehending the finality of Sonny's death. The kids were immersed in Sonny's illness from beginning to end. Nothing could change their loss but I was determined to provide them as fulfilling a future as possible.

With Sonny gone, Boobie was nervous about me holding the reins of the investment properties and told me he wanted to dissolve the partnership. Our realty trust was designed so that we both had to agree to sell. I knew I did not want to be connected to him a minute longer and saw this as a chance for a new start. I reasoned that if I chose the option of buying him out, I would have to continue dealing with the stress of tenants and maintenance. I was afraid of going forward on my own, but decided that trusting others would be even more difficult.

Predictably, both Ma and Ed were blinded by the prospect of having that much money available and were not capable of helping me make a dispassionate decision. Rowena's concern for my emotional health always colored her thinking and I already knew what decision she would suggest. In the end, I decided to sell. We received a cash offer for all the properties in one package, and the deal I had agonized over was finished in the blink of an eye. After paying off the mortgages, my share provided me with a small cushion of savings with which I could carefully guard my family's future.

The dread of winter was lifting and spring witnessed the greening of our household. Ed's daughter, Wendy, came from Australia to visit. He had not seen her in seven years, and they were both elated over the reunion. Then, other relatives and friends of Ed's from Australia stopped in Swampscott while touring the U.S. They slept on the sofas and the floors. We were crammed in, but that was part of the fun. I was happy to do this for Ed. The Aussies, with their rugged charm, actually became a force in regenerating our spirits. As part of our healing, the kids, Ed, and I flew to Europe for summer vacation. With no planned itinerary, we moved around freely for a month.

Ed was now asking me to marry him. As much as I adored him, I knew I needed to regain my confidence as an independent woman. I wanted to avoid hasty decisions and did not want to add to the regrets that already haunted me. I encouraged him to try the taxi business. I was a ventriloquist's dummy with Ma providing the voice when I began lecturing him about the business, saying that if he worked conscientiously, he could make a decent living and be his own boss. Ed experimented with the idea by driving for a local cab company, hastily bought his own hackney license and automobile, and then became thoroughly disenchanted—all within a few short months. Basically, he felt the work was beneath him. So Ed sold his taxi venture at a loss, and ran back to the clothing industry with his tape measure in hand to find work as an operations manager in a New Bedford clothing factory. He promised to relocate from Swampscott but, of course, he had no such intention and elected instead to make a two-hour commute twice a day.

Not surprisingly, after nine months of this commute, my exhausted and cranky soul mate was fired again.

The money from the sale of my property was burning a hole in Ed's pocket. He wanted me to rescue him by investing in a business he could run. I had less than zero confidence in his ability to generate the enthusiasm, provide the dedication, and devote the long hours necessary to make a new business successful. I did not take the bait. Instead, I encouraged him to show me something he felt passionate about. But he wanted the easy way out and continued to fill his time playing bridge while I was at work. We were together on my days off, but I needed more. I wanted him to take care of me, and thoroughly resented his idleness. We found ourselves at an impasse with nothing to negotiate. I still loved him, but dug deep and somehow found the courage to tell him to move out.

Forty-Two

Daddy was smoking heavily again and neglecting his health. He had regressed to his former reticence and isolation and often rode out to my house with Ma. But rather than come in for a visit, he stayed in the car with their Chihuahua and listened to the radio. If we wanted to see him, it was up to us to go out to the car to converse with him.

Poor health had impaired Daddy's judgment to the point where he now became involved in a rash of minor traffic accidents. It was obvious to everyone that it was time for him to quit driving. So, Daddy crept into bed and never got up again.

A year after Sonny's death, Ma came in from shopping and found Daddy dead in his bed. When I arrived on the scene with Ed, Ma was telling Rowena she didn't want to waste money on a funeral for Daddy, arguing, "Better that I should have the money for myself." I broke into the conversation and insisted loudly that Daddy should have a proper funeral. Rowena later pointed out that Ma was just reacting emotionally and saying extreme things. She reminded me about the Mish family's outrageous inability to deal with death and dying. But I didn't see things that way at the time, and my heated discussion with Ma broke into loud shouting and name-calling. The situation quickly escalated to hair pulling and we ended up wrestling around on the floor, stopping only after we were both completely exhausted. Rowena and Ed watched the proceedings in shocked silence, not knowing what to do, or how to stop it.

Cost was Ma's sticking point, so Rowena and I suggested that we would look into other less expensive options, like cremation or donating Daddy's remains to science. This quieted her down somewhat, and by the end of the day, when we reverted back to planning the funeral, Ma had calmed down completely and was willing to listen to reason.

Daddy's funeral was attended by what was left of the family. It was painful to watch Mucky grieve over the death of her second son. But more distressing was Ma rattling around and floundering in her own suffering. I was familiar with—and touched by—her struggle, so I invited her to spend the night at our house.

Ed departed for Canada immediately after Daddy's funeral. He had been my soul mate and companion on and off for four years. The kids, Ma, and Rowena also loved him for their own reasons. Now we were all crying for yet another loss—especially Dean, who vowed that he would never again become close to one of my suitors. I could only guess at Randee's hidden feelings, but I could still vividly remember how devastating it felt to have EIJ disappear from my young life. So Ed disappeared into another life, and I once again began the long adjustment to life without him.

Ma's one-night stay as my house guest rolled into one month, two months, and then three years. She continued to use her own apartment as a base, returning there regularly for clothes, mail, incidentals and business meetings with her tricks—yes, Ma still had her tricks. There were fewer of them, but she kept them coming, and they still paid for the privilege of being with her. Ma actually noticed Daddy's absence and grieved for him in her own way. I guess it was not so easy—even for Ma—to dismiss forty years of marriage, for better or for worse.

Oddly enough, I did not mind Ma's re-entry into my life. After all, she had always been the queen bee and I was always her faithful drone. The agonies of the last few years were catching up to me in a big hurry, and as long as I had her animated company, I was cheating the depression waiting in the shadows to ambush me.

I don't know why, but I saw it as my responsibility to keep Ma entertained and opened every aspect of my personal life to her. I *shlepped* (dragged) her to movies and luncheons and made sure that party invitations from friends were expanded to include her. She *kibitzed* (chatted) with my dates and they enjoyed her street-wise humor. I knew she could easily take care of herself, but inexplicably, the need to please her overwhelmed me. When I left for work in the mornings, I always told her the menu for dinner that night. These were not things I expected her to cook; they were things I was offering to prepare for her in order to lure her back home for dinner! In fact, I did all of the cleaning, shopping and cooking; her only contribution to the household was to sort the laundry. Ma embraced this uneven distribution of labor and apparently felt no guilt about it. Guilt was simply not in her vocabulary. And since I had absolutely no expectations for her, ours was a perfect arrangement. Her fun-loving nature and odd-ball philosophies were not lost on the kids whom she warmly showered with love and affection. She delivered newspapers door-to-door with Dean, shared hamburgers and fries with Randee and Dean at her health club pool, and taught them both the subtleties of high stakes poker.

Because we were living in such close quarters now, glimpses of the unvarnished truth about Ma's appearance and habits were starting to be revealed to us. Rowena and I had been aware of a new phenomenon—Ma was beginning to look a bit unkempt with stains often on her clothing. Previously obsessed with well-tailored, attractive clothes, makeup and a succession of blond wigs, Ma was trying to look jazzy and young, but was doing so on a very limited budget. She still had considerable flair, although her habit of stuffing her cheeks with paper to fill out her jowls—an act of pure vanity—could cause her speech to be somewhat garbled.

She was also taking nips of alcohol, in the morning, from a bottle in a brown paper bag, tucked away in her bedroom, and carried brandy in the trunk of her car to fortify herself throughout the day. At 65, Ma, nevertheless, had a small clientele of johns and a steady beau who regularly escorted her to the Saturday night dance at the Italian club. She and Auntie were members of a travel group that kept them hopping with at least four organized trips a year. Always a charismatic person, she was well-liked and accepted by her cohorts. If any of them knew her history, they certainly did not seem to care. They simply enjoyed her lively company.

I was easily seduced by my never-ending fantasy of the perfect mother-daughter relationship, and I lovingly provided food, clothing, shelter, and entertainment for Ma. Despite my largesse, I was still subject to her petty rip-offs, her lying, and her elaborate justifications. It was not that I had forgotten about Ma's silent "fuck you" while she smiled at her benefactors; it was that I never dreamed she was seeing me in that same light. I assumed that as part of her family, I was immune.

I catch Ma taking cash from my wallet and stuffing it furtively into her pantyhose. My outrage is spontaneous and dramatic, but Ma is completely unflappable and coolly disavows my accusation, telling me I am crazy. She is right; her absurd rebuttals make me crazy! Despite my hysterics, Ma does not waiver. It is common knowledge that she is a cash junkie, but I foolishly believe one of her lifelong mantras: "Never steal from your own; everyone else is fair game." She knows I never precisely keep track of how much money I carry, and she takes full advantage of this knowledge, by assuming that I will never know the difference. This is a serious and painful breach of the family bond, and I simply can't get past it. So I throw Ma out of my house, "for good."

Ma immediately went to Rowena's house and railed at my lunacy. Rowena supported me, although Ma pulled every trick in her book to convince her otherwise. This time it was Rowena who was unflappable. She calmly advised Ma to go home and lay low for a while. There followed a rash of phone calls to Rowena—Ma was calling to declare her innocence, and I was calling for consolation. Rowena valiantly tried to broker the peace, and within days, Ma was back, camping out at my house, watching her afternoon soaps, and enjoying the dinners I cooked and served. We never spoke of the incident again, but I was never able to reconcile the betrayal. As far as I was concerned, Ma's behavior and immorality had reached a new low.

During her extended stay at my house, I had been observing Ma's growing dependence on alcohol, but since I was busy with other things, I was not as aware as I should have been that she was well on her way to alcoholism. One day I discovered by chance that all the bottles of liquor I kept on hand—for all those parties I never had—were completely watered down. Without thinking, I pointed the blame at Dean and his friends. We lived just down the street from the local high school and the boys often came to the house to hang out when I was not there. But Dean denied that they had consumed any of the liquor, and I believed him. Then it dawned on me that it was Ma. She had consumed what she wanted and simply replaced that amount with water. But, in her typical way, she denied stealing the liquor. Not surprisingly, it did not bother her a bit that her dishonesty had put her grandson in an awkward position. I am sure she thought it funny.

These unpleasant episodes were yet more evidence of the strangely divided nature of Ma's feelings for her own family—especially her daughters. She didn't hesitate to tell us and others that she thought we were terrific and fabulous and was very supportive of us. In her eyes, we could do no wrong. But she always did as she pleased with little or no regard for our feelings or with any sense of loyalty to the family. In her mind, if she wanted something, she took it without regard to whom it belonged, and that was that. This attitude, like other aspects of her character, always mystified me.

Dale
Nursing School Graduation

Dale, Ma

Part Four

The itsy-bitsy spider
Climbed up the water spout.
Down came the rain
And washed the spider out.
Out came the sun
And dried up all the rain.
And the itsy-bitsy spider
Climbed up the spout again.

Forty-Three

When all is said and done, the time I prayed for is finally here. My children laugh, have fun, and our home fills with friends, joy, and music. I am in charge now. Ma is not calling the plays for me, and Sonny is no longer an all-consuming worry for all of us. I feel stronger and more self-reliant.

A decade had passed between Sonny's first seizure and Ma's decampment from my house. Now it was time to find out who I had become during that ten-year-long maelstrom. It was a chaotic nightmare-filled struggle, but I knew I had grown in the process. My plus column now contained three important accomplishments: I was able to support my family as a respected professional; I managed to avoid marrying a man I loved but who would certainly have led me to another marital train wreck; and my children were beautiful, accomplished, shining *menschen* (people having admirable characteristics) who deserved some simplicity in their lives. After Sonny's death the three of us took one day at a time, lived in the moment, and kept an eye on the future. We were a great team! I was leading a normal life and satisfied to just experience some happiness. Of course, my list had a minus column, too. Just as Ma had broken every rule of parental behavior, I had broken a lot of them too. I bore Ma's strengths and weaknesses equally, and my children saw it all.

As a single mother I was well aware that there was no one to bail me out if I failed. I became a master of frugality and ran a tight ship, not wanting to become stretched financially. But, I did not scrimp when it came to the kids' needs or the food we ate. I honed the art of living large on less. Frills such as manicures, hairdressers, and housecleaning help were out of the question. And, I had plenty of *shtick* (foolishness). No restaurant soft drinks allowed with meals, which would run up the bill. When we went to the movies, treats were purchased at sundry stores rather than paying inflated concession prices.

I became very skillful at shopping in discount stores. My family was always fashionably dressed and our house was attractively decorated. I found satisfaction in the knowledge that, unlike Ma, I did not shoplift, steal from my children, run out on dinner checks, steal a worker's hard-earned tips, max out my credit, or ruin someone else's credit rating.

I wanted my children to have adventures outside our small world, and we traveled as often as I could afford. On Christmas vacations we headed to Florida, Santo Domingo, or Mexico. We even went skiing. As long as I could sit in the lodge by a warm fire reading a good book while the children were skiing, I was happy. They got a kick out of *schlepping* me around the funky and retro stores of Greenwich Village and SoHo on our New York City trips at least two or three times a year. And Broadway theatre was always a priority. Both Dean and Randee in their high school junior years went for six weeks to live on a kibbutz and tour Israel. They were becoming the world citizens I hoped for.

Despite our many difficulties in the past, I considered it important that the kids love and enjoy Lillian, their grandmother, and thus did not turn my back on her. I included her at their special events, and occasionally, she took them out for lunch and shopping. Unfortunately, she drove away much of their affection by complaining that they did not call her or love her enough. Mel was another story. He could have seen Randee and Dean any time he chose, but he never called or showed up. I never understood how he elected to lose touch with his brother's children. After not hearing from him for ten years, they were surprised to receive an invitation to his daughter's wedding—a pleasure they decided to decline.

During this transitional period of my life, I found that living in an affluent bedroom community was sometimes emotionally difficult because I was often jealous and intolerant of many of the women there. It seemed to me that they led easier lives than I and exuded a sense of entitlement. Because I wanted to belong to their society and didn't, I often ridiculed whatever was important to them. Ma had always envied and resented women whom she believed never had to *fardrai dem kops* (worry about survival), and she often claimed defensively that women like that were dull and envied her zest and confidence.

There were moments when I, too, assumed a tough, cocky demeanor and deliberately set myself apart from other women. I remember a fashion show at a conspicuously exclusive clothing store where I could not afford to shop. I breezed in from a tennis match wearing my fur coat dramatically wrapped around a tennis outfit. I couldn't find an empty seat, and boldly stepped up front and stood next to the proprietor to watch the show rather than standing in the rear of the store. I was Ma's daughter, and just like her, I was preening for the crowd.

As I was about to enter my forties, I was aware that I was often viewed by other women as a threat. After all, I was young, attractive, energetic, and available. There were times when I briefly considered the propositions of neighborhood husbands who guessed that I was an easy mark, but always decided to avoid such liaisons. Confused about my own identity, I decided that I should work instead on establishing a comfortable, relaxed guise, to be seen as "an old shoe" in the community, which would appeal to married couples rather than just men.

But I was realistic enough to know that in order to find acceptance in the social world I sought, I had to be married or committed. The drawback was that I was completely unsure of what kind of man I could or should be with.

I started dating the vice president of a major women's fashion house who lived in Manhattan. He was wealthy and sophisticated, had been married four times, was irascible, and as Rowena reminded me, not particularly attractive. Once he was out of my life, my dating life continued in a desultory fashion. In addition to having Ma as my role model, I had stumbled into the sexual revolution and was "running with the bulls" like many other young women. I had "mini-marriages" without the commitment with several affable Tom, Dick, and Harry's and a few *meshugoyim* (crazy people). But, there was always something that prevented a serious attachment.

One hilarious moment occurred when one of my dates brought Dean and Randee unsolicited ice cream sundaes. Dean said to him, "Thanks, but I guess I won't be seeing you again 'cause Ma doesn't like you." For me, dating could often be described as, "ill-fitting shoes that blistered the backs of my heels."

"Choose me, choose me!" Oh, how I hated the moments when I felt desperate for male companionship. But I knew that any strong man would want to be head of our household, and I was not willing to move over for that. My children came first and a stepfather disciplining them would have immediately rallied me to their defense. That wouldn't have made for harmonious living. They had been through enough and I wanted to protect them from more stress. On the other hand, I wasn't interested in men who didn't want the traditional head-of-the-house role. What I needed became clearer and I didn't see my identity or worthiness only through a man.

I cherished our peaceful evenings at home. After dinner, the kids did their homework and watched TV. It was not unusual for them to shut off the lights because I, the "merry widow," fell asleep early while reading in bed. Wednesday was "Dynasty" night. The festivities of viewing and critiquing the flamboyant TV soap were accompanied by special desserts (hot fudge sundaes, baked Alaska, pie a la mode). On occasion, we would invite the most die-hard fans to share our ritual.

My concerns ran deep that there weren't any significant male figures in the kids' lives. Randee had me but was Dean participating in enough "male activities?" So, I tried to fill those shoes whenever possible. I took him on deep sea fishing trips, amongst a bunch of beer drinking guys who didn't intimidate me, and to baseball games. I used my *chutzpah* (nerve) to contact Bruins' management to ask if he could meet the players after the game. Dean, proudly carrying his autographed hockey stick out of Boston Garden, was the envy of many. When he needed to hand-carve a race car model for a boy scouts' contest, I sought a neighbor's help. His son lost the competition while Dean won. Go figure! I did everything I could to enhance my kids' experiences. Whatever the circumstances, I was a fierce lioness protecting her cubs.

In addition to my confusing dating life, I began to realize that nursing was not the right profession for me. The long hours, poor salary, layers of bureaucracy and tons of paper work had made the nursing profession less and less attractive. I still valued my nursing education and admired the dedication of my fellow nurses and the uncelebrated mettle of health care providers. I was embarrassed to admit my disappointment in a profession I had worked so hard to achieve. As I thought about my ability to support my family, I realized that I wanted to be at home more and available for my kids. However, I was not yet ready to throw away my education, so I registered with a per diem nursing agency and a secretarial bureau to achieve more flexibility.

Among my many experiences, I received a prestigious six-month assignment at Children's Hospital to work with the renowned pediatrician, Dr. Berry Brazelton, in his developmental research clinic. When my contract ended, he offered me a full time position. I was flattered and stayed on for a while but decided to pursue medical sales. However, I was advised to first acquire sales experience. My first gig was with a company owned by Hershey Foods, offering complimentary coffee makers to businesses in exchange for their monthly orders of coffee and related products, like water coolers and portable refrigerators rentals. It didn't matter that I detested coffee, had to make cold calls, and was convinced the competition's less expensive products were just as good as ours. But, I reasoned that I was acquiring experience, a good salary, and benefits. I could make all my calls in the morning and be available when the kids came home. I lasted in this job for two years, was promoted to senior sales representative, and given the task of training the incoming rookies.

Next I found a job with a New Jersey home health care company which was attempting to establish itself in New England. The AIDS epidemic was increasing the demand for home infusion therapy and I accepted the challenge of carving out a presence for the company in an enormous territory. I was on the job about two weeks when my sales manager resigned and was not replaced. Corporate sent word that I should stay on and do the best I could on my own. I was isolated once again with the task of more cold calls and trying to open an extensive territory. It was a hard sell, but hardship had never stopped me before. My old pattern of working alone served me well in this job, but, ultimately, the erratic follow-up by the company resulted in its failure.

Forty-Four

My daily habit was to walk at 5:30 am before getting ready for work. It was a hot, August morning, and I was walking briskly while listening to music on my headphones. When I reached Red Rock on Lynn Shore Drive, I sensed the presence of another person close behind me. I turned my head and found myself looking directly into the wild eyes of an enormous man. In a split second he grabbed me from behind with one arm around my neck and his hand over my mouth. I was thrown violently to the ground and dragged down the flight of stairs leading to the beach. I felt certain he was going to kill me.

Abruptly, he inexplicably let go of me and ran off. My neck ached and my arms and legs were badly scraped. I was shaky, but stood up and started to walk to my car to get away. Suddenly, another man was running towards me, shouting, "Do you need help?" Both he and the attacker were black and, in my confusion, I assumed they were accomplices in this crime. I screamed, "Go away! Go away!" By the time I reached my car, the police had been called, but I was too agitated to wait for them.

When I got home, I told Ma what had happened. She showed little reaction, so I figured I was making a mountain out of a molehill. Just as I did every other morning, I showered, dressed for work, helped Randee get ready for day camp, and drove her to the bus. But by noon, when my sales calls were finished, I suddenly burst into tears. Shaking and crying uncontrollably, I headed home. That evening, I forced myself to go out and casually related the morning's incident to my date as if it were no big deal. At midnight, the police tracked me down and came to the house to take my report. I agreed to go to the station house the next day to work on a composite drawing of the attacker.

Eventually, the police arrested a twenty-eight year old former University of Massachusetts student who had a long and violent history of rape. Then I learned that the man who called out to me to offer help was delivering the morning papers when he saw the assault. He shouted and scared away the attacker. His quick action saved me from being raped.

Months later, in front of a jury, I came face-to-face with my assailant. To my surprise, the defense attorney required a complete explanation of my job and a detailed description of the outfit I wore on the morning of the assault. Clearly, he was looking for a way to accuse me of being provocative and inviting the attack. I had to continually remind myself that I was the plaintiff and not the accused. Then the defendant's girlfriend testified that he was in bed with her on that morning.

I was asked if I recognized the perpetrator. At that point, I caught a glimpse of his mother, seated in the back of the courtroom, shaking her head and mouthing the word "No." I was extremely scared of possible repercussions against me or my children. I said, "I am not sure."

The defendant walked out a free man.

About a year later, I ran into the District Attorney who told me that my assailant had been convicted of raping other women and was finally in prison. But the event was still very much with me. Walking had been my solace for a long time, but now I was afraid to even go out alone. It would be years before I could finally lose that startle-reaction when a person approached me too quickly or suddenly came too close. An older man, with whom I shared a nodding acquaintance, heard about the attack and kindly volunteered to keep me company on my walks. We walked together for eight years and stayed devoted friends until his death.

There is a piece of dark humor in this story that still makes me laugh. When the incident occurred, I had been wearing a police whistle around my neck to blow, long and loud, if I ever needed to summon help. After the attacker fled, I blew it all right. But, I was literally so breathless from fear that the only sound I could get out of that whistle was a pathetic peep!

I don't know if the assault had the effect of finally tipping my psychological state over the precipice, or if I was an accident waiting to happen. When I had my first major depression, accompanied by anxiety attacks, it was clear that I could not get out of the hole by myself. It hit while Randee was away at overnight camp and Dean and I were home alone. I felt shaky, out of my skin, and questioned everything, believing that anyone else would have made far better choices than I.

I wondered if I had finally gone crazy. I had no answers. By sheer will, I forced myself to function while disguising my growing irrationality. For a time, I could be distracted, but eventually, anything could trigger a bout of deep despondency. I was crying constantly and embarrassed to tell anyone except Ma and Rowena. They were as frightened for me as I was for myself. One day, I wandered aimlessly around downtown Boston, unable to think straight and lost in a sense of futility and hopelessness. At times, I rambled on and on about something, sounding like a drunk. I realized I could not cope on my own and sought help.

My psychiatrist decided that I did not need hospitalization, but that medication and weekly therapy would help me climb out of that low place. I resisted, worried that the anti-depressants would brand me as a defective person who needed medication just to function. I felt flawed my whole life and didn't need another piece of evidence to prove it. The use of anti-depressants had practically become a fashion statement in the country by that time, but it made no difference to me that enlightenment was changing attitudes for the better. All the bad feelings returned that were attached to the stigma of being Ma's daughter, along with the pain of being cast out of the Girl Scouts, separated from Karen and Barry, and other friends by their disapproving parents. I was reverting to poor little, defective Dale! I didn't want anyone to know enough about me to hurt me again, but I realized this was an untenable position. I was willing to try anything that would help. So, I agreed to the meds.

The medication caused my blood pressure to become erratic. More than once, I pulled my car to the side of the road before passing out. Or, if walking and becoming light headed, I grabbed onto a telephone pole so as not to fall down on the street. Once I fainted in a department store, bringing down an entire rack of clothing. Trial and error pharmacology ultimately produced the formula that meshed the meds with my physiology. Finally, with few side effects, my anxieties eased and I slowly got my adult life and persona back. I no longer struggled to shove *little Dale* back into a dark place in my mind. I could now make sense of my inner struggles.

Forty-Five

In my random search for a suitable work life, I began to think of ways I could actually take control and become the author of my own destiny. I wondered if I dared to test myself by calling upon my creative drive and desire for independence and start a business of my own. I knew, like Ma, I had energy to burn, *chutzpah* to spare, and a powerful desire to do well—certainly not in Ma's business, but in one that was right for me! I narrowed my options to three choices. I knew something about—shopping, preparing food, and taking care of people. I thought about how these could be translated into a business and wrote a list in no particular order: 1) Open a clothing store; 2) Open a sandwich shop; 3) Start a personal services business. I briefly took a sales job in a downtown apparel shop to see if I liked that kind of business. But one day of folding sweaters and waiting for customers to come in produced an easy answer to that question—too much tedium! I realized that I might be a bit too aggressive for that setting. After all, I would not be beyond dragging in customers off the street when sales were slow.

Next I researched the idea of opening a sandwich shop in, or near, a densely populated area—like a college campus—and talked at length with Sonny's cousin who was a baker. He candidly described the demands of the retail food industry—up to and including the need to move my bed into the shop. I quickly skipped to option three. That done, I went to a business counselor at Boston College to learn the next steps. He asked me, "Where is your business plan?" My response was not surprising, given my lack of experience. I said to him, "It's in my head." Undeterred and gutsy, I simply decided that the best I can do is get something started and see where it takes me.

I had been watching the trends in the late '80s during which a burgeoning Yuppie population provided a new demand for personal services such as shopping and errands. With minimal start-up costs and flexible hours this business could be just the right one for me.

I knew I needed to create some sizzle through the print media, whose approving articles I hoped would bring me some customers. First, I contacted newspaper editors to inquire if they had any interest in doing a story about my successes. I asked my friends to pose as clients and talk about my virtuosity as a personal shopper. This is where Ma's training in the art of skillful deception came in quite handy. My friends were convincing enough for me to receive flattering coverage in several newspapers. One editor was intrigued enough to want the experience of one of my tourist shopping sprees. She brought along a photographer and later wrote a column about her jaunt with me. I found her a great suit and accessories to buy. These articles produced the clients I didn't have when she interviewed me! Shopping with other people's money proved to be not only a fun pastime, but a source of income as well.

By now, I had an idea of what I was doing, and could explain it to myself. That seemed like enough encouragement to continue. I appointed myself CEO, marketing guru, salesperson, accountant, and operations manager. There was no need for a human resource department, since I was my only employee. I produced a pamphlet featuring the newspaper coverage which gave me credibility as a shopping guru. I hoped the unprofessional appearance of this first foray into advertising would go unnoticed by potential clients.

Once I had my foot firmly wedged in that door, I took on a new emphasis: corporate event planning and the entertaining of out of town executives' spouses. It might have been a stretch, but I was selling a new and possibly exciting concept to businesses who could afford it. Nothing could hold me back.

My initial plan was to offer excursions that combined shopping and walking tours featuring stops at unique eateries sprinkled in and about historic Boston. I took books out of the library which outlined Boston's history, extracted information, wrote little presentations, and then dragged Ma along with me to listen to my spiels while we stood at the sites. Her companionship made my doggedness fun. Evenings were spent typing and memorizing the notes I had scribbled by day. I took whatever tours were available to observe other guides in order to polish my showmanship. Eventually, with Ma's approving review of my performance, I anointed myself a full-fledged tour guide.

The task of defining and learning my job was lofty. I worked at home during this startup period. But I did not want to give myself the chance to slack off just because I was at home. I dressed up every morning in a tailored suit and heels just as if I were going to a business office, had muffins and conversation with a breakfast group at a Marblehead coffee shop, and then returned to my office.

Cold-calling in previous jobs enhanced my growing repertoire of job skills. All those years of juggling competing priorities as a mother, the wife and caretaker of a terminally ill man, and training to become a professional nurse, had given me the ability to cope exceedingly well with a lot of clashing responsibilities. I felt undaunted by the difficulties. I was a budding entrepreneur!

Little by little, I started investing in professionally-designed brochures and business cards. Dean cleaned and painted the cellar, and I officially moved from my kitchen table to the basement —along with my dilapidated desk, old sofa, and coffee table—into my World Headquarters. The humming of my washer/dryer provided the reassuring background noises that might have been provided in a regular office by the low buzz of office gossip. Rowena bought me a new computer and printer in celebration of my grand opening, but I had no idea how to even turn it on. However, it certainly looked official.

My business strategies were only guesses and I floundered around a good deal, unearthing information from any relevant source I could. I was learning the new language of business. How would my proposals translate into revenue? Ma said, "Think with your head, not with your ass." Graceless words, but I got the point and knew I would figure it out as I went. I must have been either nuts or fearless—or maybe a little of each—and started calling upon hotel sales directors in order to introduce myself as the new kid on the block, the lady who could dazzle the hotel's out-of-towners. I pointed out that while there were other operators who planned tours and events, my hook was to offer "hands on" attention and superior service. *Oy!* Fortunately, at that stage, no one was interested enough to ask me for any nitty gritty details, and I was still fishing for a plan.

After my strategic sales attack on the hotels, I boldly walked into the Department of Harvard University's

Continuing Medical Education Program. I knew I was entirely out of my league, but was nevertheless filled with excitement and psyched about carving out my future. The department was planning to offer a national seminar in the spring, and I boldly proposed that I could design and produce tours for their attendees. They listened, and then invited me to submit a proposal. I rushed from Harvard directly to Rowena's office for help. She offered resources, hand-holding, and proofreading while I invented and constructed my first proposal.

Harvard read my suggestions and became seriously interested in my offerings. They told me the next step was for them to judge my competency as a tour guide extraordinaire—firsthand! I decided to offer them as my trial tour, a behind-the-scenes visit to Symphony Hall followed by presentations at a couple of trendy South End art galleries. I dug deep for all those bits and pieces of recently accumulated knowledge and found that pounding the pavement with Ma, the gallery hopping, the food tasting, and the travel reading was still in my memory bank. Two of the Harvard administrators came along on the tour with several paying customers. Rowena knew how nervous I was, so I padded the group size with her office staff, and she herself came along to silently cheer me on. Then the most amazing thing happened—I got the Harvard gig!

With that victory ringing in my ears, I visited Sylvania Corporation. They were planning a big-league sales meeting. I must have seemed confident and experienced, because somehow I walked out of that meeting with an order for fifty gift baskets, some busing responsibilities, and a commission on any of my excursions the spouses signed up for. I was shocked and scared—but ready! I got busy composing the tours, and then booked professional guides who were far better prepared than I was to lead them. I called a bus company and set up a schedule. When the day finally came, I was so antsy that I went to the garage to personally sweep out the buses. I had absolutely no idea how to charge for all these services, but somehow I arrived at an acceptable figure and even managed to make money on the deal.

Paine Webber's Investment Division in New York was preparing a multi-day meeting to be held at a Cambridge hotel. The sales department had expressed interest in my approach to tourism services and recommended me for the off-site activities—a clambake at the Aquarium, a private dinner and boat cruise on Boston Harbor, and two daytime tours. I was completely dumbfounded by this avalanche of good fortune and promptly took to my bed, overcome with insecurity and doubt. Suddenly I was telling myself that I would surely screw this one up, and my deficiencies would be cruelly exposed to a whole new population. With all the affection of doting female elephants, Rowena and Ma sat at my bedside trying to calm me. Nothing made me feel better until Rowena called my bluff by suggesting that I should just sell the job to a competitor for a percentage of the gross profit. She knew I couldn't tolerate giving up a huge chance like this. So I promptly shed the jitters and dug in. As a complete neophyte, I made some pretty amusing *faux-pas*. For instance, I didn't know if the Aquarium had electrical outlets and asked the manager if I needed to bring generators for the band's equipment! Nevertheless, I was on a roll, and would never suffer a crisis of confidence again.

I was learning a new language—proposals, conventions, meeting planning, catering, busing, tours. I would figure it out, no matter what it took. I joined The Boston Convention and Visitors Bureau which offered leads for upcoming conferences.

The business was now a very important part of my life and I was successfully servicing meetings, large and small. Each client had different needs and specific requests which posed brand new challenges. Some required guests to be shuttled all over the city. Others asked for a dinner reception accompanied with music and entertainment. Potential clients would call and ask if I could put together such events as a 5K run on the banks of the Charles River, followed by a breakfast. Others would ask if I could arrange a color guard for an opening ceremony. My portfolio of successful custom-made events was growing steadily. I was definitely on a roll.

Finally, I put a label on my vision—it was a *Destination Management Company*. There was plenty of competition out there and I had to continually search for a way to make my company stand out from the growing crowd. But, G-d knows, I had a flair for the dramatic, and didn't have trouble adding a creative edge to my proposals. Of course, I couldn't do it all on my own. There were too many details. I eventually hired a wonderful support staff to assist with all aspects of marketing, sales, operations, and tour development. Together we made the business a success.

Soon, many of the corporate offices that initially waved me off were starting to call me and place orders for services. Some needed me to provide activities for foreign clients whose international flights required an extra day's stay. I found myself escorting people from all over the world, most of whom spoke little or no English. On one such occasion, I drove around Boston with a delicate, kimono-clad wife of a Japanese executive. With little else to talk about and my nonexistent knowledge of Japanese, I decided to teach her a few English words. I feel sure she had never met anyone like me and suspect I might have offended her sensibilities while I shouted out words at the top of my lungs that she never asked me to teach her. It was pretty funny.

The Police Chief of Cairo did know English, however. Our day together was to be spent in the midst of a four-day heat wave, and I greeted him in a sleeveless dress with a mid-thigh hemline. He recovered nicely from his jaw-dropping gape and agreed to let me stop off at home to pick up my son Dean, who was very interested in meeting a court official from another country. Dean stepped out of the house wearing shorts and a tank top with the words *Temple Israel* embossed across his chest. Clearly, we were pretty clueless, but the Chief was a good sport and overlooked our lack of sensitivity to his cultural and religious biases. Maybe it was even a good thing for him to meet a Jewish mother and her son and learn that we were just regular people. During our time together, we had lunch at a Boston watering hole, talked politics, and found bargains for his wife and daughters. I was sure he had fun!

I was also interested in developing a market for presenting history to locals, so I added weekend tours in Boston and its surrounding towns to the mix of services my company provided. The idea was to furnish reasonably priced cultural opportunities and take care of all the driving and logistics that would be necessary. That third component of my company needed a catchy name. Rowena aptly suggested *Urban Safaris*.

The success of the local tours encouraged expansion into diversified day trips around New England and New York. Soon some of the area colleges were listing my trips in their Adult Education catalogues. When this happened, I quickly promoted myself to the positions of head writer and editor-in-chief of *Urban Safari's* newsletter which reached out to the general public and advertised all my seasonal offerings. My safaris were all working so well that colleges asked me to conduct seminars and lectures on the tourist industry. One college asked me to join their board to help develop the curriculum for a program in tourism and hospitality they eventually implemented.

I tried hard to give my clients the best value for their time and money. There was an encyclopedia of details that could have gone wrong, but fortunately not many did. I was diligent and lucky. The business was my baby that I lovingly doted upon and I am still amazed at how far I was able to take it in order to achieve both gratification and satisfying compensation.

I find that working on the buses, providing tours and supervising drivers a throwback to my family's experience in the cab business. Was my drive to create my business somehow tied to that unaccustomed view of my father when he was briefly happy, recounting an enthusiastic, but often inaccurate, commentary on the sights and history of Boston?

Forty-Six

Ma stops communicating altogether and sleeps most of the day. I get into her bed, hold her in my arms, and start prattling on about all of her favorite subjects: the kids; who I bumped into at the supermarket or at Marshalls; what everyone was wearing, who they were with, and how poorly they are aging. She cannot respond, but I feel her body relax completely as I murmur the gossip in her willing ear.

For months Ma had been complaining about leg pain. It did not prevent her from taking a two-week trip to Spain in 1990 with Auntie and their travel club, but the problem was bad enough for her to arrange for a wheelchair to use on the trip. The two sisters had their usual good time, but when the plane landed at Logan Airport, Ma had to be taken to a hospital emergency room in Boston. She was suffering from excruciating pain, and this time she couldn't ignore the problem.

Rowena went straight from her office to the hospital where she and Ma passed several hours talking about Spain and catching up while waiting to hear what the X-rays would show. The doctors decided to admit Ma for further tests, and a few days later they told us the cancer had eaten away most of her thigh bone and spread throughout her body. We looked at each other quizzically. Cancer? What cancer?

Ma, who had never hesitated to let us in on every sordid aspect of her life, had ironically been obsessive about keeping her knowledge of the cancer a secret. It had started as vaginal cancer years earlier, but she had chosen not to tell us because she didn't want to risk losing her independence. At the same time, she also decided unilaterally not to seek treatment. Her attitude was summed up in one memorable explanation, "I didn't want to be tied to a hospital. I wanted my life on my own terms, so I rolled the dice. I'd either get better or I wouldn't. No hard feelings, whatever G-d gave me, I'd take." But she didn't get life on her own terms. She had cancer. It would dictate the terms.

So Ma took what G-d gave her and never complained to Rowena or me, and made only a few slip-ups that would have alerted us if we had been looking for them. With the usual hindsight, we recalled several times when we overlooked an obvious clue to her developing condition. One of those was a time when she spent a weekend at Rowena's house as cat sitter. When my sister came home, she noticed there were little drops of blood around the house. Rowena assumed one of her three cats had been injured and duly inspected all twelve little paws. Finding nothing, she forgot the incident. Another time, I found rust-colored stains on my white rug and scolded Ma for spilling her ever-present brandy. She played the game and apologized for her carelessness. How unlike her! She never apologized for anything. But still, I didn't pick up on the fact that she was dripping blood around my house.

Then I flashed back several years to a day when she told me she fled from her doctor's office because he wanted her to submit to a test. When I questioned her then, she was vague and defensive. Always neurotic about anything medical, she stonewalled me and I stopped asking questions. In retrospect, I surmised he probably detected a problem during a Gyn checkup. Ma instantly put the problem into her denial machine. I assume that her fear conveniently morphed into anger at the doctor and she never went back to him.

No surprise—Auntie knew all along about Ma's illness and did not tell us. Shame on her! Her inseparable bond to Ma precluded all common sense—even in matters of life and death. Ma had already let the teeth rot out of her head rather than see a dentist. Now, rather than cooperate with a doctor, she had opened the door and invited Death to come right in.

When Rowena and I went to see her at the hospital, she often did not want us to stay long because she was expecting Morris. When I was 14, he became EIJ's replacement for awhile. Now, years later, he was back and had been her companion for some time prior to her illness. Although it touched raw nerves that Morris' company was preferable to ours, we couldn't help but feel secretly relieved. His presence took the burden off us and allowed us to continue our lives. I believed it was Ma's way of not wanting to tie us down by sitting at her bedside. The devotion Morris showed her was extraordinary.

An orthopedic surgeon strongly recommended immediate surgery to repair the damage in Ma's thigh bone. He was the first doctor to propose any proactive treatment and showed us an X-ray of her thigh. He warned that if the bone splintered, she would be permanently bedridden. Ma was very reluctant—probably terrified—about having an operation, but eventually agreed to it.

Hers was a nasty recovery from the surgical intervention and we could see that it had been a poor decision. We had been angry at Ma for not trusting us enough to tell us about her illness. But now we realized guiltily that our first and only involvement in her treatment had caused her to suffer unnecessarily. A lousy patient, Ma rejected physical therapy, and even refused to get out of bed. We saw that she settled into the hospital environment and acted as if it was her personal retirement community. She ate three hospital meals a day, entertained visiting friends, and in the evenings curled up in bed to watch her favorite television programs. Just like home!

Rowena and I visited the hospital every day, sometimes together, sometimes independently, and listened to her wacky tales of torture by the nurses. We tried to motivate her with tidbits designed to soothe her soul. We brought her a boom box and tapes of her favorite Klezmer music and sang with her the Yiddish songs she loved.

When I went to the hospital early mornings to bathe Ma and fix her hair, she often threatened to get a "real" nurse to attend her. We laughed at the joke, but I could see that the cancer was destroying her spirit. She was becoming more and more unmanageable and chided every nurse and therapist who approached her. Then, about two weeks after her unsuccessful operation, Ma was transferred to a chronic care facility in Cambridge which also served as a hospice. The new oncologist told us, "Operating on the femur was useless; the cancer has rotted away almost every bone in her body." To say the least, this was a dire revelation.

Rowena's communication with Ma is almost telepathic. She fixes her eyes on Ma's for a few seconds and answers Ma's unspoken question, "Yes, Ma, I bought a dress with the birthday money you gave me." Ma closes her eyes and imagines the dress while Rowena describes it. At age seventy-three, our mother is dying.

For Rowena and me, the sun burning out in five billion years is a more immediate possibility than the notion of our mother's death.

The first week in hospice care was consoling because, unlike the hospital experience, the staff simply let Ma alone. But by the second week, she was shutting down, eating only a few bites, sleeping most of the day, and quickly losing the ability to speak. We could see that she had had enough. All she wanted now was a quick, pain-free ending, so she signed the necessary hospice document with no argument from us. Ma's life expectancy had melted down from weeks to days to hours.

Rowena sat very quietly with Ma as she slept fitfully. Suddenly, Ma became extremely agitated and looked around the room, terrified. Rowena gazed into Ma's wide-open eyes and said in a quiet voice, "It won't be long now, Ma." Then she held Ma's hand while she drew her last breath.

When it is all over, Rowena and I stare at each other. Who will we be now? Our mother had ruined our lives just as she had defined them, and we can't imagine life without her. I spent my whole life casting out her negative influence and absorbing her brow beating lessons only to realize in the end that she gave me a gritty strength to fight my way through trouble and hardship while making countless errors in judgment along the way. I both loved and hated her for who she was and for what she had done to and for our family. We laughed together, survived together, and fought each other to exhaustion. She callously sacrificed Rowena and me in order to save herself. She lied to me and stole from me, and then sang and danced with me as if nothing bad or perverse had ever transpired. Of the characteristics she left us, I know I have her fervor and fire, and Rowena has her strength and stability.

Ma was certain that no one would show up for her funeral, and cited her reputation as the underlying reason. She would have been amazed to see how many people attended. The rabbi even expressed astonishment that someone her age had such a large turnout. We chose to have Klezmer music playing in the background as the people came in to visit us before the service. The crowd included some local cronies Ma had hung out with at her health club, friends from her Saturday night dance group, buddies from her traveling club, Auntie's friends, my friends and Rowena's, and, of course, Morris. Maybe even a trick or two showed up, although we had no way of knowing that, and undoubtedly some of the people who had once scorned her were now paying their respects.

The service passed in a blur, except for the ray of sunlight that suddenly broke through the unusually mild winter day and shone through the window directly onto her casket, placing the spotlight directly on Ma, where she would have wanted it. Afterwards, Rowena and I settled into the funeral limousine and smiled at one another. So many people, so many cars, such a nice eulogy—it was Ma's idea of a great party!

Now that I am a grandmother of five, I can see, as never before, that I have broken the cycle that Ma set in motion all those years ago. I am no longer a prisoner of the past.

At his bedtime, my little grandson Max asks me, "Nana, what does gottenyu mean?" "Maxie," I say, "It is me telling G-d how much I love you." When I play with my Benjamin, Jordan, Brooke, Sophie and Max, I do the things I always yearned to do as a child.

While I do so, I remember wonderful Moishe, the only adult who encouraged me to enjoy playing. My grandchildren and I gather rocks and shells and come back to my deck to paint them. We go apple picking, bake cookies, and play hide-and-seek. At the amusement park, I drive one Dodg'em car and Benjamin rides with Dean in another. We laugh wildly as we crash into each other.

Jordan, Brooke, Sophie, and I play tea party with their dolls, attend library programs, and enjoy stories and crafts. We go to museums, the zoo, puppet shows, and playgrounds. We ride the swan boats, and visit Mrs. Mallard and her ducks in the Boston Public Garden. When we shop I put them in a cart, dress them in hats and scarves, and accessorize them with purses. We hide from their mothers, and scoot up and down the aisles giggling.

As I put these beloved grandchildren to bed, I lean over them, put my hands on their little backs, shake them gently, and chant: "I love 'em, I need 'em, I want 'em, I have to have 'em, no strangers can have 'em, they're mine, they belong to me. He's (or she's) a shaineh (beautiful), he's (she's) a bubeleh (term of endearment), a kindt (child), the velt (world) and I love you forever."

One day, when Randee is tucking in Jordan, she starts to say my chant and gently shakes Jordan with her hands on her back. But Jordan tells her to stop, "because that is what Nana does." And that is how I know that although I have broken the pernicious cycle Ma started, some of the good things remain of my mother. This is one of them:

"Come, I will say my words to you as I tuck you in. Wouldn't you rather be in your bed than anywhere else?" Ma is rubbing my head and making low guttural sounds, and finally, I find the comfort I have been seeking.

Epilogue

My beautiful and charming daughter Randee—who has a heart of gold— acquired a Masters Degree in Broadcast-Journalism from Northwestern University. After succeeding as a television Anchor/Reporter in Arizona, she returned to the East Coast as a reporter for a Hartford, Connecticut TV station. Bobby, a terrific young man, lured her back to Arizona, where they married and are raising Jordan and Brooke, their daughters. Randee teaches Communications at a university.

My handsome son, Dean—kind and generous—graduated from the University of Miami Law School and passed the Bar. With two partners, he established a bond trading firm. After eight successful years, their firm was purchased by a major bank. Dean has a wonderful and devoted wife, Marcie, and together they are raising a son, Benjamin, and twins, Sophie and Max, and my grand-dog, Otis, a golden doodle.

Rowena retired as Chief Financial Officer of a noted college, after serving there for many dedicated years. Single sex marriage is legal in Massachusetts, and Rowena married her partner, Pam, several years ago. They live within minutes of my house. Rowena continues to be involved with numerous friends and activities. She wrote lyrics to a friend's musical composition and for many years, participated in and choreographed for a senior tap dancing group. Currently, she plays poker, sings with a choral group, and conducts seminars for gay seniors. When I started the process of writing this memoir, she tirelessly made outstanding contributions. It was quite a journey for both of us.

Auntie Helen retired to Florida and passed away after suffering many years from dementia. After Ma's death, she never mentioned a word about how much she missed Ma and all the things they did together. The only thing Auntie asked for after Ma's death was the oil painting of Poco the Chihuahua.

Ed and I lost touch many years ago.

Billy, still living in the Boston area, was unwilling to speak to me when I called his sister for his phone number and an update of his life.

After twenty extremely rewarding years running my destination management company, I retired. I met the whole world at my doorstep and was grateful for the achievement and independence I gained. Despite the demands and challenges, it was a lot of fun and I would not have traded the experience for anything. It was a treasured gift.

Since dating for me was like "trying on many ill-fitting shoes that caused lots of blisters," I finally got the fit right and married a *mensch* (a gentleman, a fine person) in 1993. Saul, a widower with three grown sons and six grandchildren, came into my life at a time when I was finally ready to share the joys of companionship. Not only is he a very intelligent MIT "techy" graduate," but as a retired electrical and software engineer, he assisted me in expanding my business. He automated my office to the point where I wouldn't have been surprised if he loaded one of those computer buttons to perform cooking and cleaning chores. We are very fortunate to have traveled all over the world and enjoyed great times. Even after private tango lessons in Buenos Aires with a tango master, he still can't do the dance but neither can I! More importantly, he makes my life significantly happier. He is just a lovely, lovely man.

I was once jealous of the neighborhood gals who belonged to the Swampscott Beach Club. They seemed to enjoy such privileged and carefree lives in comparison to my own. I could not afford the membership. Eventually, the beach club was torn down and condos were built on that property. Saul and I bought one of the units and now enjoy having the ocean right outside our door.

I have friends and a rich social life. However, in my heart I remain a loner who listens to a strong inner voice. I have managed to control occasional recurring bouts of depression with medication, and occasionally visit my psychiatrist for well-being check-ups. After forty-five years, I am one of her longest-standing patients. She was an extremely important and wise mentor to me in my journey. I credit much of my growth and stability to the guidance and understanding she offered me.

Rowena and I returned to 1333 Blue Hill Avenue a few years ago to revisit the tiny apartment where we spent our childhood and where so many memories—often difficult and unhappy—were spawned. The landscaping that used to surround the building has been mostly torn away and a chain link fence and a dumpster littered with graffiti mar the building's outer appearance. The rooms seemed even smaller and darker than either of us remembered, and the yard and fire escape—once the site of our play—seemed hopelessly small and inadequate. How odd that these tiny rooms and tiny yard had been the site of such outsized experiences. My mind keeps traveling back to that place over and over, year after year, searching for reasons, for feelings, for the truth of what happened there so long ago.

I survived, garnered strength, and learned to thrive from all the trials and experiences. I love my life and family. The good which has happened to me looms very large. Thank you, dear G-d.

Who would have ever dreamed!!!

Acknowledgements

I am indebted to my dear and trusted initial readers, Maureen, Jon, Don, Richard, Paul, and Sheila who provided extra eyes and helpful critiques; to Sylvia and Pam, special friends offering their wise opinions; to Tansy Blumer who helped organize and clarify my writings, to Karen Lateiner for reviewing the manuscript, and to Carol Nadelson for her never waving guidance and excellent advice.

This memoir could not have been brought to fruition without my husband, Saul, who not only designed the front cover, but whose immeasurable cheering on and timeless efforts helped me to fully grasp the power of my story and its potential to encourage others to overcome adversity; my wonderful children who showered me with their love and approval; and Howard and Erin, for their encouragement to continue when my resolve was waning.

www.TheHookersDaughter.com

TheHookersDaughter@Gmail.com